Richard William
Bledsoe

Can Saul Alinsky Be Saved?

Can Saul Alinsky Be Saved?

Jesus Christ in the Obama and Post-Obama Era

RICHARD WILLIAM BLEDSOE

WIPF & STOCK · Eugene, Oregon

CAN SAUL ALINSKY BE SAVED?
Jesus Christ in the Obama and Post-Obama Era

Wipf & Stock
An Imprint of Wipf and Stock Publishers
199 W. 8th Ave., Suite 3
Eugene, OR 97401

www.wipfandstock.com

ISBN 13: 978-1-62564-788-7

Manufactured in the U.S.A.   12/04/2014

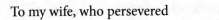

To my wife, who persevered

We can only be restored to sanity by the Most High God.

Contents

Introduction | ix

1   Hebel | 1

2   Personality | 19

3   Ethics | 26

4   Can Saul Alinsky Be Saved? (Or, Should Saul Alinsky Go to A.A.?) | 32

5   God Speaks, Therefore I Am | 58

6   A Couple of Paradoxes | 75

7   The Proofs | 88

8   The Kenny Letters | 108

9   The Uniformity of Nature and Biblical Authority | 118

10   Origins and Truth | 125

11   Who Is This Man? | 130

12   Afterword | 137

Bibliography | 141

Introduction

My most interesting ancestor is my paternal grandfather, whom I never met, and is therefore unsullied by actual memory. He has taken on something like mythic proportions in my own soul, and he stands in purity for things that I now believe are better fulfilled by looking up rather than looking either to the left or to the right. Who he was became, in a less purified form, a generational hope for both my generation (the "60s generation"), and then later, my own children's generation.

My grandfather was essentially a frontiersman who grew up at the edge of the close of the West. He was killed in 1947, several years before I was born, when his automobile turned over and he was burned alive, returning from tending to his beehives. The honey he harvested from them was a part of his earnings. He and his family scratched out a living in a small town in southern Colorado. From all reports, he was a force to be reckoned with. My father told me that in the years before, he fled to Colorado from Texas where he was a farmer, and had shot off the kneecaps of two lawyers who had stolen his land through "legal shenanigans." My father also told me that he had won third prize for the use of a handgun in the Texas state fair in 1906. "And there were a lot of gunslingers in Texas in those days," he added. The Ku Klux Klan ran and essentially controlled Colorado through much of the 1920s and 1930s. They had a great deal of power in his small town. Even though it was suppose to be a secret, it was well known that the owner of the hardware store was actually the Grand Wizard of the local Klan. My grandfather was a vocal critic of the Klan, and they threatened to come and burn a cross on his front yard. He went down to the hardware store and bought a Colt .45 from the owner. The owner asked him what it was for. "Well," he said, "if those Klansman ever come up to my house, they will find out." They never came.

On another occasion, there was a local election, and it was made known that Catholics and Hispanics were not welcome to vote. My grandfather went and stood, just stood, next to the ballot box, and then sent my uncle and father all over town in his Model T Ford, and they picked up Catholics and Hispanics all day and brought them down to vote. Nobody interfered.

My grandfather was not only a man who could take a stand; he was also, unusually intelligent. When my mother was very old (approaching one hundred years old) I asked her for some of her memories of him. She said, "He was tall and seemed very important. Whenever we saw him, he always gave us a lecture that seemed to last for about an hour, and I hardly understood anything that he said."

"What did he lecture about?" I asked.

"Philosophers."

"Which ones?"

"The only one I can remember is Socrates," said my mother.

Apparently, he read everything. My father told me that he taught himself mathematics all the way through calculus. I still have some of his mail order correspondence-school textbooks in my library. All of this was from a man who did not have a high school education, and often had to work as a common laborer to make a living.[1]

Four years before the Russian Revolution, when my father was born in 1913, my grandfather named him after the author of *The Communist Manifesto*.[2] My father's first name was Marx. You do not give your son such a name unless you think a very great deal of the namesake in the first place, and he espouses what is your ideal. I have no doubt my grandfather read, not only the *Manifesto*, but also *Das Capital*,[3] and had a very good grasp of what Marx was saying. He was a lifelong socialist, and my sister has in her possession some of his correspondence and writing that he left behind that display his convictions.

I get the impression that Saul Alinsky and my grandfather would have gotten along very well. They seemed to have a lot of the same Leftist ideals. They were for the poor, the underdog, the left behind, and they wanted them to have the power to make their lives better. Saul Alinsky (1909–72) was a "community organizer," who gave his life to promoting tactics to confuse, divide, and dispirit the enemy, who was always the American

---

1. My grandfather was also a self taught chemist who set up a laboratory in one of the buildings on his property. He worked for a local paint company that produced lead based paints.

2. Marx and Engels, *Communist Manifesto*.

3. Marx, *Capital*.

Establishment. He wanted to take power from the "haves" and give power to the "have nots." His most famous book is called *Rules for Radicals: A Pragmatic Primer for Realistic Radicals.*[4]

There was a time when only a small circle of political activists knew Saul Alinsky. But in recent years, he has led a ground swell. Part of his resurgence can be credited to Barack Obama, the 44th President of the United States, who was and is a disciple of Alinsky. As a community or- ganizer in Chicago, long before he ever thought of the presidency, Obama taught seminars on Alinsky, and led demonstrations that were based on his tactics. He brought much of that to his own presidency and tenure in the White House. Alinsky is a thinker who has written some things that impinge on the contents of this book; Obama is mentioned very scantily in the text. The book is not about Obama, and only impinges on him as he is a carrier of Alinsky's theology. He has carried forward some of Saul Alinsky's philosophy and he has injected it further into the public mainstream than it has ever been before in the relatively conservative United States. The United States has traditionally been the least secular of all Western Nation-states, a fact noted as long ago as Alexis de Tocqueville. America is now catching up (if that is the correct term) with the far more secular European nations, and Obama is very much the representative figure of coalescence. He is an especially representative figure of late or post-modernity, and it has been broadly noted since the 2012 election, that America is more nearly now two nations than at any time since the Civil War.

The Obama and Post-Obama Era represent the second triumph of what are now commonly termed "the 60s." It is that environment that this small volume addresses; however, that environment began long, long ago. It actually began in the Garden of Eden, and it has been breaking out ever since. It seems to be the natural bent of the human race. This is not a book of political philosophy, and you will be disappointed if you are looking for

---

4. In the chapter entitled "Tactics," Alinsky promotes thirteen rules that have since become infamous. Here they are: 1) Power is not only what you have, but what the enemy thinks you have. 2) Never go outside the experience of your own people. 3) Wherever possible, go outside the experience of the enemy. 4) Make the enemy live up to their own book of rules. 5) Ridicule is man's most potent weapon. 6) A good tactic is one that your people enjoy. 7) A tactic that drags too long becomes a drag. 8) Keep the pressure on. 9) The threat is usually more terrifying than the thing itself. 10) The major premise for tactics is the development of operations that will maintain a constant pressure upon the opposition. 11) If you push a negative hard and deep enough it will break through to its counter side. 12) The price of a successful attack is a constructive alternative. 13) Pick the target, freeze it, personalize it, and polarize it. Alinsky, *Rules for Radicals,* 126–30.

a detailed critique or examination of Saul Alinsky's works. Rather, it deals with issues that are very much prior to politics. Theology used to be termed "the queen of the sciences," and whether known in our age or not, theology is still the queen. Saul Alinsky begins his most famous book with a theological affirmation, and it is that affirmation that is basis of all that this book examines. Alinsky dedicates his book to the author of the first rebellion. He dedicates the book to the memory of the rebellion of Lucifer.[5] Much of modernity has its origins in doubt and in rebellion. The names of Descartes and Rousseau, among others, set our steerage in the direction of a declaration of independence from heaven, and the myth that doubt, revolt and self assertion are the ultimate values that will lead to an ascension into glory, and a final kingdom of man, or of youth. Saul Alinsky is the latest American incarnation of that faith. It is clearly an apostate faith. Can he be saved? Can even Saul Alinsky be saved? If so, then there is hope.

I admire much of what my grandfather stood for: I admire his courage, his fearlessness, his care for the underdog, the powerless, and the poor. But I now doubt his map. I am not sure my grandfather believed in an ultimate origin or destiny. To quote G. K. Chesterton:

> In short, the modern revolutionist, being an infinite skeptic, is always engaged in undermining his own mines. In his book on politics he attacks men for trampling on morality; in his book on ethics he attacks morality for trampling on men. Therefore the man in revolt has become practically useless for all purposes of revolt. By revolting against everything he has lost his right to rebel against anything.[6]

One has to believe in something before one can doubt anything. One has to obey somebody or something before one can revolt against anything else. The devil has no ground on which to stand to stage his revolt, except the ground that was already created by another. He can in the end only stand for nothing. His nihilism, his nothingness, can only result in vanity and vapor. I am not sure that my grandfather did not in the end come to share my own doubt of doubt. He came to join the Mormon Church along with his family, for at least a period of time. That is a chapter that has always been mysterious to me, and he did not live to explain it to me, nor did my father explain it to me, who died an open unbeliever. My grandmother, who died when she was 103, wanted to return to the Hardshell Baptists of her

---

5. The details and documentation for this can be found in the chapter 4 of this book.

6. Chesterton, 47.

Missouri childhood, and my uncle was befriended by and I believe brought into the fold of the believing, by a neighbor who was a Bible-believing Seventh Day Adventist, before his death in his eighties.

This book is largely a defense of speech, but it is above all a defense of the reality that there was a speaker who preceded the insinuations of doubt and rebellion, who is still speaking. God was the *first* speaker to Adam in the opening scenes in the Garden of Eden, and Lucifer, who was an interloper, was the second. To be human is ultimately to hear God and to speak to God. We were in the first place spoken into existence, along with our entire environment in our world and universe. God's speech is the origin of all that is, and if we grow deaf to that speech, eventually we cease to hear anything, and all meaning disappears. We are turned over to the false hopes of the Lucifer referred to by Alinsky. God's speech is to be found in final and full form (in this world) in the most common place of all household items: the Bible. It is everywhere, and it is easy to find, but increasingly, it is almost unknown. It is however, the secret of existence, the open sesame.

The modern world is in some "official" sense, afflicted with unbelief. Modernity is almost synonymous with unbelief. And yet a great deal of the "modern" world, especially in the United States, is not modern at all. Many people who are in the most obvious and superficial sense, contemporaries, are in fact "distemporaries."[7] That is, the assumed official ideology of the age is not shared by many, many people of our age. Many people are still in the mindset of nineteenth-century revivalism, or Reformation thinking, or even in many ways medieval. A world of angels, archangels, sin, redemption, and answered prayer from the hand of an omniscient, omnipotent God are not in the least foreign to millions of "modern" people.

I have been a Presbyterian pastor in a university town rather well known to broadly partake in modernity in a pretty deep way. In some ways, my town is more an outpost of the mindset of Western Europe than of the American West. I am personally a "distemporary" of most of the people around me—so were the members of my small church, and the several thousand other evangelical believers in this area. And yet I find that being a "distemporary" does not at all inhibit or destroy the ability to communicate with those around me. In fact, in some ways, it enhances communication. It is, after all, sometimes more fun to talk to an outsider who has an utterly different perspective on the world than to speak with those whose opinion

7. I owe the term "distemporaries" and the idea that the word represents to Eugen Rosenstock-Huessy. See especially *The Christian Future*, 172.

is already known and almost entirely shared. Over the years, I have fostered the habit of offering to pray for my "distemporaries" when they have become good enough friends to let me in on some of their troubles. I have never had one person refuse me, or treat me as though my sanity ought to be checked. Quite the contrary, I have always been treated with the utmost of seriousness, and with great appreciation when I have offered such prayers. I even encounter what seems to be a kind of hopeful belief. They seem to really believe that if I pray, something will happen, and it often does. They often say, "I can use all the help I can get." It makes me believe that unbelief is not as absolute as some modern thinkers, and curiously, theologians of a particularly modernist stripe would like us to believe.[8] It has led me to believe that something like a breviary of unbelief might even be helpful to certain modern people. One has the impression that many unbelievers are utterly ignorant about why they do not believe. It seems to them to be as certain as was the flatness of the earth in Columbus' day, or the Ptolemaician order of the stars prior to Galileo. It is in other words, an unexamined premise that simply functions from day to day. And yet when it is challenged in any existential way (for example with an offer to pray for conflicts or problems), it doesn't seem to offer much resistance or be very absolute. It might pay to examine it. It might pay to see if there is some viewpoint that might offer some surprising light on it.

If there is a God (which these people seem implicitly to be open to), what might God's point of view be on the fact that there is so much unbelief in and about God? Does God have anything to say about it? I began to examine this question several years ago trying to understand the unbeliever not from his own perspective, but to see what the Bible itself has to say on the subject. Personally, I have found unbelievers own account of their unbelief to be mostly a blank, or a series of denials that are not very illuminating. In my experience, God is very illuminating when he speaks concerning any given subject. Most people don't know this because they only know the Bible on a most casual basis, and have never studied it on almost any question.

I hope to give some illumination—the kind of illumination that even my grandfather would have found to be another, and better, kind of enlightenment.

8. It is ironic that it is especially modernist "theologians," like Bultmann or Tillich, who are the quickest to assure us that belief in a supernatural Gospel is virtually impossible for modern men. Bultmann's quip that since we have electric lights and radios, men can no longer believe in God is an especially telling, and silly example.

1

Hebel[1]

SOLOMON WAS REPUTEDLY THE wisest man in his time. Solomon's last discoveries had to do with the utter emptiness and vanity of the world. He wrote an entire book about it. "Vanity, vanity, all is vanity," is among the best known literary statements in the entire world. If understanding or experiencing this statement implies wisdom, or at least a great prelude to wisdom, then the modern world must be pretty nearly the wisest age in all of history. A vast number of modern people have soundly declared this to be what they, too, have learned out of life. At first blush, they do not appear to be proud, for they say it is all there is to be learned. For volume, this is pretty slim in terms of philosophy. It appears to be a kind of humility. But it could be a species of pride as well. The nature of pride is that it lies, especially by means of inflation. It believes very small things to be very big, especially if it is about ourselves or our knowledge. Solomon could have been humble (because he knew what a small thing nothingness really is), and the modern world, claiming the same thing, could be proud—swelling nothingness to a very great and vast thing.

It is curious that modern men and women have learned what a vast thing the universe really is, and have commonly declared how insignificant we as human beings are. It is, at the same time, declared that almost all of that vastness is absolutely nothing as completely empty space. The odd thing about this new and startling discovery of vast amounts of nothingness is that it seems to have had an effect on our own view of ourselves. It seems that more of nothingness (if that makes any sense) renders us less significant than less of nothingness used to. The deep oddity is that this, far

1. *Hebel* is the Hebrew word variously translated as "emptiness," "wind," "vapor," "vanity."

from being a mournful conclusion that has been ruefully and regretfully reached, is rather a delight to a large number of people and has been embraced as a positive liberation. How can this be? Does this indicate a great and swelling pride at being modern masters of a great deal of nothing? Does it indicate a kind of masochism at taking so much enjoyment in having been rendered utterly insignificant? Are we perhaps not so much like Solomon after all? Are existentialism and nihilism really another beginning and not linear descendants of Solomon at all?

It might be good to return to Solomon, and see if he did say anything that is different from modern pride. We might learn something. Solomon's perspective seems to be that the world is very little, even "nothing" only because God is very great. To be proud of "nothing" was something that Solomon seemed to be past, and at great cost to himself. It was, in the end, not an excuse for self-infatuation, or the exercise of power, or for the lax practice of any and all kinds of eroticism. All of that had been tried and found wanting. Indeed, those very things are part of the vanity of this world.

Solomon was a forerunner, a kind of John the Baptist, of the great idol cleansers of several hundred years later. In a global fashion, iconoclasts rose up at the four corners of the world. Loa-Tse in China, the Buddha in India, and Socrates, the ironic debunker in Greece, all arose at almost exactly the same time. All of them decried the nothingness and folly of the gods. None of them, however, made claim to know the true God, the one who was "I Am Who I Am, and I Will Be What I Will Be" (Exod 3:14). To provide this positive element, we find the prophet Isaiah in Israel, the one who is really Solomon's successor. The other three iconoclasts became self-conscious about the nothingness and were among the first "unmaskers" in world history. But they either left this nothingness as something to be realized as final, or in the case of Socrates, tease and hint at somebody or something beyond it but still unknown. In some ways, they were perhaps close to the modern purveyors of nothingness like the existentialists or the nihilists. Isaiah was the true successor to Solomon, and he beat them all to the punch by maybe three hundred years. He had a great deal to say about nothingness in the life of the people of Israel in his own day. The people were deceived. Unlike Solomon, they were not wise about nothingness, but, more like modern people, were very foolish and proud about nothingness. They did not recognize the nothingness as nothingness, but proudly believed it to be the most wonderful and substantial stuff there ever was or ever could be. They believed that which was really nothing to be actual gods; they worshipped the gods of nothingness. But Isaiah declared this: "Indeed you are nothing, and your work is nothing, he who chooses you is an abomination" (Isa 41:24). He says this sort of thing over and over.

The difficulty that Isaiah faced with his people was a paradoxical one. They wanted gods that could be seen, and imagined the visible to be the real, or the most real. But God declares himself to be Jehovah, the Utterly Substantial One, or the Self-Existent One, and he is invisible. This was a considerable stumbling block for the people. How can something or someone who is invisible be more real than that which can be seen? There is a very interesting story to be unfolded here, and one that has great bearing on who we are as moderns. It is a story worth telling again, even though it has been told before.[2]

To be called to be a prophet is not an enviable calling. It is proverbial that the prophet, who tells unpleasant truths, rarely lives to enjoy much if any satisfaction from having been right. He is usually a casualty of his own correctness, and is often literally resented to death. The Lord, as he is wont to do as the Lord, appeared to Isaiah in his regal and overpowering majesty, and called for a spokesman to come forth on his behalf. Isaiah volunteered. Apparently, only a volunteer would be called to such a difficult mission. He is told that he will go forth to preach, and that the effect of his preaching will be to render the people even more utterly stupid than they were at that time. As they hear his preaching, they will be made deaf to it. As they "see" what he is driving at, they will become morally blind. The effect will be that the people will be rendered incapable of repentance, or even of understanding. Isaiah, obviously dismayed, asks how long this will go on. God tells him that it will go on until he has destroyed the nation as punishment for its deafness to his voice and blindness to his precepts.

The story behind this is to be found in two of the psalms, penned hundreds of years earlier. Psalms 115 and 135 give echoes of the language used in Isa 6. The exact language that is used in Isaiah to describe his call is this:

> And I heard the voice of the Lord saying, "Whom shall I send,
> and who will go for us?" Then I said, "Here am I! Send me."
> And he said, "Go, and say to this people: 'Hear and hear, but
> do not understand; see and see, but do not perceive.'
> Make the heart of this people fat, and make their ears heavy,
> and shut their eyes; lest they see with their eyes, and hear

2. Barfield, *Saving the Appearances*, 174–86.

with their ears and understand with their hearts, and turn and be healed."
(Isa 6:8–10)

Psalm 115, which was written some hundreds of years earlier, is a taunt to
the Philistines and other pagan nations around Israel. It begins by extolling
the God of Israel, and then asks, "Why should the nations say, 'Where is their
God?'" In other words, the nations taunt Israel for worshipping an invisible
God. The rest of the psalm is a counter taunt to their idolatry. Of course their
gods are visible, but examine the logic and the folly of these visible gods.

> Their idols are silver and gold,
> the work of men's hands.
> they have mouths, but do not speak;
> eyes, but do not see.
> They have ears, but do not hear;
> noses, but do not smell.
> They have hands but do not feel;
> feet, but do not walk;
> and they do not make a sound in their throat.

Then comes the corker line:

> Those who make them are like them;
> so are all who trust in them.
> (Ps 115:4–8)

This has the effect of making it be the other side that looks ridiculous. Their
God, they declare, "is in the heavens, and does whatever he pleases." He is
quite alive and nimble, and not a stupid block of wood. This also has vast ex-
planatory powers. Worship, adoration, and trust have the effect of conform-
ing the worshipper to the form of that which is worshipped. In other words,
if you worship a stupid block of wood, that in effect is just what you will come
to be like. The Philistines were blockheads about matters of the Almighty.

After several hundred years, the endless war with idolatry inside of
Israel was a lost war. The Israelites, in effect, became Philistines. They, too,
began to worship stupid blocks of wood. Isaiah has a facetious heyday with
his own people, taunting them just as the psalmist taunted the Philistines
(showing the comedian at heart as a sad tragedian). Portions of chapter 44
are marvelous irony:

4

He cuts down cedars; or he chooses a holm tree or an oak and lets it grow strong among the trees of the forest; he plants a cedar and the rain nourishes it. Then it becomes fuel for a man, he takes a part of it and warms himself, he kindles a fire and bakes bread; also he makes a god and worships it, he makes it a graven image and falls down before it. Half of it he burns in the fire; over the half he eats flesh, he roasts meat and is satisfied; also he warms himself and says, "Aha, I am warm, I have seen the fire!" And the rest of it he makes into a god, his idol; and falls down to it and worships it; he prays to it and says, "Deliver me, for thou art my god!"

He then delivers this stinging indictment:

They know not, nor do they discern; for he has shut their eyes, so that they cannot see, and their minds, so they cannot understand. No one considers, nor is there knowledge or discernment to say, "Half of it I burned in the fire, I also baked bread on its coals, I roasted flesh and have eaten; and shall I make the residue of it an abomination? Shall I fall down before a block of wood?" He feeds on ashes; a deluded mind has led him astray, and he cannot deliver himself or say, "Is there not a lie in my right hand?" (Isa 44:14–20)

A generation later, during Jeremiah's tenure as prophet, the Israelites were taken into captivity in Babylonia for seventy years as punishment for their idolatry. Upon return to Jerusalem, only a few came, and many Jews became permanently, "a people without a nation." But during this time, God's chastisement finally bore fruit. The Jews never again worshipped idols. They learned their lesson. The Jews became notorious despisers of images seeing them as a true abomination.

This brings us to our strange turn in the story. By the time Jesus came five hundred years later, the Jews were even more infamous as haters of idols. But the oddity is that Jesus posits the ordination passages of Isaiah as a cornerstone of his ministry. They are quoted numerous times by Jesus. Jesus is asked in the Matt 13 why he so constantly teaches in parables, which the people do not understand. He answers using God's words to Isaiah.

You shall indeed hear but never understand,
and you shall indeed see but never perceive.
For this people's heart has grown dull,
and their ears are heavy of hearing,
and their eyes they have closed,
lest they should perceive with their eyes,

and hear with their ears,

and understand with their heart,

and turn for me to heal them. (Matt 13:14–15)

Jesus is, in other words, accusing Israel of spiritual stupidity because they are idolaters. However, the Israelites were not idolaters. They had been cured of this during the Babylonian captivity. So what is the meaning?

In a parable, Jesus said that if a house is exorcised of an unclean spirit and it goes out seeking rest, but finds none, it will return to its original abode finding it clean and swept, but empty. He will then move back in with seven other spirits more evil than himself (Matt 12:43–45). The most sensible interpretation of this parable is that during the captivity, the evil of idolatry was cured in Israel. But the cure was superficial, and by Jesus' own time, Israel was seven or eight times worse than in the time of Jeremiah. But how? The Jews abominated graven images in the time of Jesus.

The answer seems to be that something more noxious, complex, and less obvious had taken the place of simple idolatry. If idols made Israel an abomination to God, then these later developments make Israel even viler to God. If anything is clear from the gospels, it is that the leadership of Israel is extremely unpleasing to God. Phariseeism and Sadduceeism, judging from Jesus' language, were certainly abominations. They were themselves forms of idolatry.

The Pharisees saw themselves as something like the true spiritual remnant, and were above all interested in ritual purity. Nothing was more important to them than a spotless conscience. The Sadducees were Grecized Jews who had taken large doses of Greek philosophic wisdom into their own minds. The Pharisees were men of conscience, and the Sadducees were men of intellect. In both cases, simple submission to the Torah had been replaced with some form of human invention.

This is the false deification of humanity's own creative powers. What would happen if the external trappings of the block of wood or stone were removed, but the same mental projections were continued? What if mental constructs were projected and then made absolute? This is very much the case with the spiritual leadership Jesus' day. In effect, both the Pharisees and the Sadducees rejected the word of God, and replaced it with their own word and their own mental constructs. The Pharisees established their own traditions that were so powerful and all controlling, that they had the effect of completely eliminating the commandments and revelation of God. The Sadducees, Jesus said on one occasion, knew "neither the Scripture nor the power of God" (Matt 22:29). The Jewish church had broadly lost its grip on God's calling and intention for them and had replaced it with desire for ritual purity, and sterile speculation. Their entire theological system was idolatrous, and it had exactly the same effect as idolatry in Isaiah's time; it made them stark blind to the reality of God and of his works. Jesus as the very Son of God stood and acted before them, and they had no idea who he was.

Isaiah declared that not only were the idols "nothing," but those who made them were likewise "nothing." By the time of Jesus, idolatry had become a more convoluted and subtle thing, a thing that was obviously human and not wood or stone. The nub of the issue had been exposed. Idolatry was exposed as essentially worship of man, and of the self and its productions. But once humanity is made absolute, the creator and the creation of the new idol become at once the same, and both fall under the rubric of "nothing." Here is the whole essence of the truth of the Christian revelation. Outside of its acceptance, there is "nothing." Man and his world are only something inside of the sphere of belief and faith. Otherwise, man himself becomes mere wind, vanity, emptiness. He has not even enough substance left to be able to credibly oppose the truth of the gospel. The ensuing two-thousand-year history of mankind has served to illustrate this, and we shall give a sketch or two so that all who have eyes to see may see.

AUTONOMY

One of the most used words in the last two or three hundred years to describe what our modern era is about is the word "reason." The word really does not have a pedigree of accuracy, and is much more a term of evocation. Somehow it marks off "modern man" from his little brother in the so-called Middle Ages as very grown-up, and not apt to take instructions from authorities outside of himself. He thinks it all through for himself now and does not need outside supervision. The point is that it is a term that really means "autonomy," more or less.

It is hardly the case that modern man discovered reason. Aristotle knew quite a bit about it, and was very handy with syllogisms and all the apparatuses of logic. What it really has to do with is before whom or what is it necessary for man and his faculties to kneel in submission? Or, can he stand as his own king and ruler answering to no one? For almost any thinking person before the so-called modern era, reason had to work on whatever stuff was given to it before hand, and therein were limitations and potentialities determined. Out there was a world, a universe that was prior to thinking man. Some of it was visible, and some of it invisible; however, one applied the intellect to all of that stuff. Now, beginning with Descartes, man decided that in a new way he needed to grow up. He needed to leave behind the notion that our intellect works on the given, and the intellect instead needed to become creative, providing for itself its own "stuff." This is not exactly common sense, but it is this that provides most of the arrows for the modern quiver.

It is with Descartes' new beginning in philosophy that a certain transparency or clarity is given about what is really going on. Descartes always strikes me as being a bit juvenile. He boldly cuts himself off from tradition, revelation, and even the external world, and falls wholly back upon himself. He has all of the confidence of a brave but foolish adolescent in that he can entirely recreate the universe out of his own resources from the inside. First, he closes his eyes and pretends the world isn't there and plays a great game of doubt, seeing just how much he can doubt before doubting becomes impossible. He is just the opposite of the Alice in *Alice In Wonderland,* who sees how many impossible things she can imagine before breakfast, making her universe as crowded as possible. Descartes imagines how many doubts he can entertain before even imagination evaporates, trying to create as empty a universe as possible. I don't know if he did this before breakfast or not, but he finds in this game that he can doubt everything except the fact that he is and that he thinks. "I think, therefore I am." Thus, he believed that he saved both himself and thought from extinction. After Descartes discovers that his self is truly the Rock of Ages, he proceeds to spin the whole universe out of his own thinking thorax, and even manages to find a place for God in his grand scheme of things. I am not sure, but I think he did all of this in less than seven days. Therefore, we get a new bold beginning for the creative powers of thought.

The point I make in the previous section is that in reality, this kind of thing has been going on for a very long time, much longer than Descartes' development of it. It was going on in Isaiah's day; it was going on in David's time before Isaiah. In truth, even Aristotle was doing it. Jesus unmasked it when he accused his own contemporaries of not seeing what was really there, because they wanted to make up their own reality, and attributed all kinds of divine qualities to what their own minds and consciences were doing. I don't suppose it was until Descartes that the cat was really out of the bag that all of this was the self, masquerading as both creator and redeemer of all things. The "new beginning" of Descartes was only a relative step forward in consistency from past positions. This new model of the thinking self was factory-equipped with divine attributes. Before, this was also true, but much less obviously.

There is a problem with all of this, though. Isaiah declared that not only were the idols nothing, but so were those who created them. This same logic can be seen working itself out in the modern world. I have often wondered if in all of Descartes meanderings, he knew what sort of a self it was that was beyond doubt. If everything everywhere could be doubted, except Descartes and his thinking, then just *what* could it have been that Descartes was thinking about so indubitably? It seems a rather circular process; if only "thinking" and "self" are final in terms of reality, then Descartes must have only been able to think either about himself or about thinking. In either case, the effect is quite similar. The self is irreducible because it thinks. It can, I suppose, think that it thinks, but that still gives only two topics of possibility: thinking, and thinking about thinking. The self becomes indistinguishable from the thought. Descartes seems to have believed he salvaged his own existence, but he may have only salvaged the reality of abstraction. Just what the thinking is about is problematic. It seems to only be about thought itself, since nothing else indubitably exists. In this way, the thinking seems to be the same as thinking about nothing, or at least it is difficult to distinguish what pure thought about thought could be from nothing. One, in other words, gets something like a "self-thought thought," or a thought thinking itself. Aristotle, too, thought of the Self-Thought, Thought as an ultimate thing, but was not so conceited as to have in a completely bold way declared himself to be this. He imagined it to be something outside of himself that he did partake in when he thought, so Aristotle could imagine a universe that was a great deal bigger than he was, even if in the end, it all boiled down to about the same thing.[3] For both Aristotle and Descartes, however, exactly how one attaches a self with unique particular qualities of identity beyond thinking becomes a problem. The particular self with a name and an identity (like Rene Descartes), and the world that one naively believes that he inhabits, are superfluous and

3. From Aristotle's *Metaphysics*: "Thought thinks on itself as object in virtue of its participation in what is thought." The objects of God's thought must be limited to what is unchangeable and so to himself. This does not mean however, that Aristotle has produced thought with no object of thought. We should, rather, suppose that God *is* those truths which are free from change and that it is these which he thinks. Osborn, *Encyclopedia of Philosophy*, 161.

unjustifiable extra baggage. Abstraction is so sleek that attaching anything else to it as an appendage becomes a quandary. There seem to be no hooks to attach particulars to. For these thinkers, thought cannot be un-thought, but the thinkers are themselves entirely superfluous and one can never find an adequate connecting point between abstraction, the living self, and world that we live in.

We can deduce that Aristotle's Self-Thought, Thought, and Descartes' self-thought thought are really one in the same with certain metaphysical grandiosities left out of Descartes' version, and a certain level of conceit left out of Aristotle's. We can understand that both versions are themselves idols. These are not idols of stone, as in the case of Isaiah's people, or idols of tradition as in the case of the Pharisees. They are idols of thought, of rationality. Now, nakedly, the self is self-presented as a self-sufficient deity. But the irony is that with the deification of the self, the self renders itself extinct. It is a poor god who cannot even exist.

The logic of the Bible is very clearly working itself out here. Those who make idols become like them. They become insensible, incapable of seeing, hearing, or moving. They may exist, as does the idol, but the existence is not a living or aware and conscious existence. The self that Descartes theoretically salvaged is as insensible as a rock.

Since Descartes' time, a lot of moves have been made that give different versions of self-beginnings. Descartes' self began and ended by running aground with a version of reason that can never make contact with the very self that wants instrumentally to use it. So an entirely different kind of beginning that is almost the opposite of Descartes was attempted. David Hume, a Scottish philosopher of the eighteenth century, did not begin with the pure thought of the self, but rather with the perceiving self, the sensory self. He ends up, however, in a place that is adjacent to Descartes. Hume did not believe that this sensing self, which is the basis of all knowledge, had any direct sensation of itself. His language indicates that he inferred a self, since he constantly referred to himself as the recipient of sensation; however, Hume did not believe in the reliability of inference since he could not sense an inference. Descartes believed only in the power of reason to be the illuminator of all else. Hume doubts the power of reason to demonstrate to us anything necessary in the realm of real existence. All that exists that we can be sure of is that which can be immediately known as parade of sensations. Hume cannot directly discover Hume, and doubts that he exists. Hume says:

> For my part, when I enter into what I call myself I always stumble
> on some particular perception or other, of heat or cold light or
> shade, love or hatred, pain or pleasure. I never, catch myself at any
> time without a perception, and never can observe anything but a
> perception. When my perceptions are remov'd for any time, as by
> sound sleep; so long am I insensible of myself and may truly be
> said not to exist.[4]

In words that are almost a parody of Isaiah's or Jesus' concerning the idol
worshipping self, Hume goes on, "And were all my perceptions removed by
death, and cou'd I neither think, nor feel, nor see, nor love, nor hate after the
dissolution of my body, I shou'd be entirely annihilated, nor do I conceive
what is farther requisite to make me a perfect non-entity."[5] Hume believed
that he was already a non-entity, but was currently burdened with the illusion of a self-existence so long as the parade of sensations continued. He
was, in other words, already dead. It is also curious that Hume doubts the
self because he would have to infer its existence, but does not flinch to infer
the self's non-existence because of the lack of immediate perception of it.
One is as much a deduction as the other.

Another new way of thinking about the self, and perhaps the most
important one for our purposes, was introduced by the late eighteenth-
century philosopher, Jean Jacques Rousseau. Rousseau was a Genevan,[6] but
France is the nation he influenced the most. His *Confessions* offers a stark
and modern contrast to the other most famous *Confessions*, those of Saint
Augustine. Augustine's *Confessions* is a book-length prayer, and offers illustrations of the opening paragraph of Calvin's *Institutes of the Christian
Religion* in which Calvin claims we can only know ourselves in the light
of God and of knowing God. Rousseau's *Confessions* is committed to the
exercise of knowing himself by means of introspection. Rousseau believes
he is sincere, perhaps more sincere than anyone before or after him, and he
is so sure of the truth of *Confessions*, that he will present it at the Last Judgment to God himself as the true record of his life. Rousseau's *Confessions*
is undoubtedly a kind masterpiece, and was hugely persuasive to the world
and people of his time, and perhaps did more to create the modern milieu

---

4. Hume, *Treatise*, 252.

5. Ibid.

6. The two most illustrious Genevans in the history of that city are counter opposites
of each other, and each represent outlooks that are diametrically opposed. The first is
Rousseau; the other figure is, of course, John Calvin.

than any other single book. He was an enormous literary success. For Rousseau, the way to salvation for the self was through the doorway of feeling.

What is meant by "feeling" is not so easy to define. It certainly involves knowledge. Being unavoidably at least stepchildren of Rousseau, we will often say, "I feel" this way, or that way, and in part what we mean is, "I think." What it really involves certainly has intellectual or cognitive content, but it is also an evaluation or judgment. "I feel depressed," is not just a descriptive phrase about one's feelings, but also about a state of affairs that stand outside of us that we are connected to. It is a judgment on the world around us. "Today is a depressing day," is a value statement, and a judgment on the world outside of me, but through my own internal emotional state and consciousness. This is distinctly modern. This is a world created and evaluated through my own feeling states. This is not *per se*, a bad thing. Humans are clearly meant to be co-creators of the world, and our feeling states are an intrinsic part of our personhood. Rousseau, however, was committed to grounding his personality ultimately in himself, and of knowing the reality of that self by feeling his own existence. Augustine is no less subtle and no less subjective. He knows himself in conversation with God, and is suffused with the Bible. For Rousseau, self-knowledge is a result of autonomous self-love.

Rousseau distinguishes between *amour-propre* and *amour de soi*.[7] *Amour-propre* is the source of all itching, writhing, psychic misery. It means that I see myself through the eyes of others. More simply put, it means, I live in fear of what society thinks, or feels about me. I view myself with fear, fearing that I do not cut a sharp enough figure in society to be loved. My energies go toward making myself loveable. Society is turned into a popularity contest in which I can be one of the "in" ones. The world becomes a junior and senior high school, with the quest to be king and queen of the prom. I can only love myself because others love me and regard me as worthy.

Amour de soi is the quest to love myself apart from the opinion of others. I will make myself worthy by means of my own act, and that act is primarily a quest for "sincerity." Rousseau's entire *Confessions* is an attempt and an exercise to escape *amour-propre*, and remake himself by means of *amour de soi*. He begins his famous *Confessions* with what is surely one of the most easily satirized paragraphs in all of the history of literature; he vows to be more sincere than any writer before him has ever been. Rousseau is the great-grandfather of all of the writings of all of the silly schoolgirls in all of the yearbooks of all of the schools that ever were.

7. Grimsley, "Rousseau," 220.

Dear Alicia, What a glorious year it has been!!! What I just love about you is how sincere you are!!! Love, Susan

Of course, Alicia, knowing that sincerity is the great ideal, has spent all year working very hard at not only feeling sincere, but affecting it to everyone around her. Sincerity is only in the most vague way an ethical ideal like the ideals that came before it, but it is still an ideal. It is meant to be a feeling, and through this feeling, one will come to self-knowledge. Rousseau felt very sincere in all that he wrote, and was very impressed with his own literary production at the end. He was sure he had written the greatest book that had ever been written.

What he means by "sincere" is that he will report without dissimulation, his own feelings about himself and his life to the reader. But one should note that what he sincerely feels about himself may not be the same as what is plausible or true to anyone else. One might be sincerely self-deceived. Rousseau believed that he could be sincere about himself by loving himself, by affirming himself. It is precisely here, however, that so much of the modern condition is explained. The two *amours* together form a dialectic, with one ricocheting off the other. I am not sure that it is ever possible to escape from one to the other. The paradox is that in the very act of writing his *Confessions*, he is writing them (which are meant to be an act of *amour de soi*) for the public, and they are an act of brazen self-display. He cares very much that the public admire him for his daring and bold self-revelation.[8] In other words, the book is an entire act of *amour propre*. In attempting to escape the opinion of other people, he runs headlong into caring for nothing else. He wants to be considered the most sincere man who ever lived, and he will flaunt it even in the face of God.

The contradiction that we have stumbled upon is that, oddly, "sincerity" is the very same thing as hypocrisy. Rousseau, in claiming to be the most sincere man who has ever lived as early as his opening paragraph, is surely committing one vast act of dissimulation. In saying, "I do not care what anyone in the world thinks of me," Rousseau is really saying, "I hope I am more admired and loved by society than anyone before me or after me, in my unprecedented boldness in claiming not to care."

---

8. This includes his bold revelation that he successively gave all five of his children by his mistress Theresa, to foundling homes. "I thought I acted like an honest citizen, and a good father, and considered myself as a member of the republic of Plato." Rousseau, *Confessions*, 307.

13

S. W. Orwin, in his introduction to Rousseau's *Confessions,* refers to Canto LXXVII of Lord Byron's *Childe Harold's Pilgrimage*:

> Here the self-torturing sophist, wild Rousseau,
> The apostle of affliction, he who threw
> Enchantment over passion, and from woe
> Wrung overwhelming eloquence, first drew
> The breath, which made him wretched; yet he knew
> How to make madness beautiful, and cast
> O'er erring deeds and thoughts a heavenly hue
> Of words, like sunbeams, dazzling as they past
> The eyes, which o'er them shed tears feelingly and fast.[9]

Byron notes what we might now call the neurotic self-destructiveness of Rousseau. If the normal course of life does not provide sufficient misery, it becomes necessary to create something like self-affliction.

In Rousseau, we especially find ourselves awash with so much that is modern. There is bathos, sentimentality, and the relish of pity that has its origin in self-pity. He nearly succeeds in making the self absolute as the feeling self, and then very quickly loses that same self as it drowns in its own self-felt concern. He is lost in self-pity and in self-importance in petty tragedy. Anything can be a tragedy—a toothache, the smallest unrequited love.

Rousseau didn't invent anything absolutely new. He simply placed an emphasis on certain aspects of life that had never before been given such importance. Everybody has always known about feelings. Bathos and sentimentality have been around for a long time, but mostly as comedy. Rousseau made self-concern, in a deepened way, the end of life; for literary Europe, however, he managed to make it respectable. The importance of romance is not the glory of the beloved. The importance of romance is the glory of my own feeling of being in love. He was in love with being in love, and the beloved is a really quite secondary self-extension. He glorified the self's importance by making the smallest self-pity seem as immense as the tragedy of King Lear.

What Rousseau accomplished was a lineage that is very old, and is deeply tied, ironically, to the love of death. The final glory, one begins to suspect, would be suicide over the tragedy of a toothache. Hopefully others will notice. My tragedy makes *me* overwhelmingly notable and important.

---

9. Ibid., 2–3.

Does one ever escape *amour propre*? If God is not my *final* audience (the world is our proximate audience) I have no one through whom I can truly know myself. I need an audience. *Amour de soi* is an impossibility. I, therefore, become a hypocrite—not wanting a God who sees leads to *amour-propre* necessarily, and therefore, hypocrisy. The feeling self is finally a self that extinguishes itself. It is a self that establishes itself through its own beautiful and tragic death, to be noticed by others. Rousseau is the original modern narcissist, the foundation stone of the great and burgeoning industry of psychiatry.

With Rousseau, one is not so much dealing with the smell of the academy, and one is certainly not dealing with precise and rigorous arguments. But there is an order and logic of the feelings that work themselves out. What is worked out in the end is self-extinction through self-absorption. Oddly, the more we feed our self-esteem, the more we despise ourselves, and the less we are affirmed. Here, we see the Democratic man as opposed to Aristocratic man, self-esteem as opposed to aristocratic contempt as a basis for self-affirmation. But self-esteem is really the failed attempt of the democratic man not to despise himself, as the aristocrat had despised the commoner before. But oddly, he can, in the end, only feel his own existence through self-contempt, which he then deals with by means of projection outward unto others.[10]

Who was this lover and this beloved inside of Rousseau? Is this one who feels love for the self, sensing a prior self, or does he create this self? Did Rousseau exist before he felt himself in love, or did this love create this person?

There is a manifest contradiction here. Rousseau makes a good deal of "virtue." The self is a "virtuous" self. But Rousseau is very interested in maintaining the utter independence of his existence. This good or virtuous self is only good because Rousseau loves this self. He creates himself by loving himself, and makes himself "virtuous" because he loves himself, and then "feels" this self-creation. He, in other words, creates himself out of nothing. Did he authentically exist before he loved himself? Where was he before he discovered this love? Apparently nowhere. He did not exist. Then he who did not exist began to exist and brought himself into existence by love. But how? By loving himself. Unfortunately, there was no one there to carry out the act

---

10. This projected self-loathing is the source of the sniveling smallness seen by Nietzsche that he termed *ressentiment*.

of loving. Which is prior: self-love, or existence of the self? One cannot be without the other. This is creation out of nothing, *creation ex nihilo.*

What if one does not feel oneself, or what if the feeling is extremely tenuous? What if the principle feeling one has is one of complete emptiness? What if there is no one there to "love?" Does one cease to exist, or did any one exist in the first place? Can something then be artificially layered on top of the emptiness besides self-love to reassure oneself that existence is real? I have heard reports recently of some of the young people in Europe who have become a part of an underground occult and satanic movement glorifying pain, and even reveling in the thought of damnation in hell. "Why?" asks the inquisitive and baffled onlooker. One commits oneself to pain, because if one has pain, one "feels" one's existence. It is better to be in pain, but feel assured of existence through pain, than to experience oneself as complete emptiness.[11]

This can take a lot of avenues, and most of these are very modern sounding. The term "neurotic" is thrown about a lot in the modern world. Its meaning is not very precise, but there seems to be a ballpark of reasonably similar connotations and definitions. A neurotic is one who is constantly offended, and the offense is self-manufactured and then projected onto others around. Hence, he can never be pleased. In the modern world, it is better to feel grief and offense, even if imagined, than to feel nothing. This feeling of grief and offense also connects one to other selves. One can "feel" the reality of other selves, even if only negatively. It is a sort of "anti-relationship." Perhaps even existing in perpetual hostility with others is preferable to not existing and being completely alone in not existing. Or, even more absurd, the one thing that many people share is a feeling of slipping existence, which ends in endless talk about one's own neurosis and one's therapy. If one is not going to exist, it is preferable to not exist in company and among others.

The United States—my own country—is, at this moment, in grave danger of falling into a final and irreversible sinkhole of Rousseauian sludge. Some years ago, the American education system adopted the "middle school" philosophy, which replaced the old-fashioned junior high school. The purpose of junior high was quite simply to prepare students for high school; the purpose of high school was to complete a basic and foundational educational curriculum that would enable one to enter the work and domestic force of the country, and also prepare some of those students for higher education at the nation's colleges and universities. One, in other words, had

11. Glasser, *Reality Therapy*, 99.

to submit oneself to a particular body of learning. However, by the 1970s and 80s, America had been extensively psychologized. The purpose of education for adolescents ceased to be submission to a curriculum for life preparation, and was replaced with collective therapy to enable students to develop a "healthy self-esteem." School, in other words, became "student-centered," making the development of the students ego the central reality. The student, then, no longer submits him or herself to something larger than and outside of themselves, but the entire educational establishment submits itself to them. School became "ego-centric" in the most literal way. This was the essential purpose of middle school as opposed to junior high.[12]

The middle school is an entirely Rousseauian institution, and has built into it all of the contradictions and conflicts that are outlined above. Not surprisingly, it has, over time, issued in all of the above contradictions. This phenomenon surely has contributed (it cannot be the sole cause, but is surely in concert with the entire cultural sump) to a massive increase—perhaps even an epidemic—of narcissistic personality disorder.[13] Narcissistic personality disorder is nothing more or less than what happens to people who are taught that the goal of life is *amour de soi*, but who have no means to achieve this outside of *amour-propre*. In other words, if God cannot be one's final and ultimate audience (as with Augustine in his *Confessions,* who gave himself to, but did not pander to, a public), then one can only "play to the crowd" as with Rousseau. The result is a world of constant offense, extensive hypocrisy, and a societal "anti-covenant" in which harmonious relationship is nearly impossible. In short, the Rousseauian "middle school" philosophy is a recipe for a completely neurotic society, one dominated by psychiatry and a legal profession with an inordinate number of people involved in lawsuits over absurd and petty offenses. What should have been a passing moment in the development of the adolescent's personality in junior high school (with the constant sense of seeking to be "in" and "popular") is now elevated to the final meaning of life and as grist for an everlasting therapy mill. It is a recipe for an adolescent society in which everything coalesces around *nothing*.

The dilemma for Rousseau, and for the modern world following, is much the same as for previous thinkers, but has perhaps a more existential logic that has less the odor of the academy about it. When "I" feel, does "my" feeling prove "my" existence? Do "I" feel myself, or is any feeling merely a

12. Twenge, *Generation Me*, 17–103; Kilpatrick, *Why Johnny*, 13–128.

13. Campbell and Twenge, *Narcissism Epidemic*.

pure perception? Is it the "self-felt feeling?" Is the pain "pure pain," abstract pain that is unconnected to any other personal existence?

Do I really exist, and does anybody notice?

2

Personality

THE ACCOUNT OF THE world proposed by modernity and postmodernity is a contradictory one. The question that needs to be raised is, what accounts for personality? This is clearly not a ridiculous question with an utterly self-evident answer, yet if the assumptions of the modern world are true, this must be a self-contradictory, and therefore absurd, question. It is viciously circular, because in almost all accounts of modernity, personality itself is treated as a self-defining first principle that accounts for everything else, and yet there is nothing in the modern world that is weaker or more in constant need of propping up, and healing, and remaking from outside sources than personality. Personality appears to be not very self-sufficient. In its most extreme and absurd forms, this contradiction takes the mode of modern philosophers or scientists writing whole books that purport to reduce consciousness and the sense of personhood to chemistry and exploding electrons, thereby reducing the act of people writing books for other people to read to a complete Chimera. Personality researches, thinks, speaks, writes, and publishes for a broader community of persons in order to prove that such things as researching, thinking, speaking, writing, and publishing are things that cannot be done because there are no truly conscious persons to do them. There is only chemistry and exploding electrons that have the illusion of doing them. Here, however, even the illusion has no explanation. Human personality, which is the origin of all things, does not even exist.

These books become ironic, because every year the explanations they offer in explaining away consciousness become more complex, and there is the illusion that a very complex materialist answer to the problem of consciousness is more persuasive than a simple materialist answer. Complexity is a different category than coherence, though, and I think the authors are sometimes too clever for themselves, being tricked by their own massive learning. A book of this sort with a great deal of learned micro-biology, physics, organic chemistry, and cybernetics, is no more persuasive than a book written as a joke that begins, "Dear Reader, you may think you are reading this book, but you are not."

It may well be that philosophers have committed intellectual suicide over the last three or four hundred years, but what about the "man on the street?" Why should he care? Even amongst philosophers, we find David Hume for example, chucking philosophy when it becomes too strange, and restoring himself to "real life" with a good game of backgammon. There is a case to be made in two directions concerning what intellectuals do. Some people argue that intellectual x writes completely incomprehensible book y, and one hundred years later, everything is different because of that turgid book. For example, when Karl Marx's *Das Capital* began to filter into Russia, the censors saw no harm in allowing it over the borders since it was such a technical and boring book that nobody would bother to read it. Apparently, the censors were entirely wrong! Other people, however, think that intellectuals are much more a mirror of the social milieu and do not influence it so much. However that may be, it is clear that by the twentieth century, and into the twenty-first century, this is not just a philosopher's issue. Personality has grown rather thin for the "man on the street."

Psychiatrically, schizophrenia is the mental disease of the disappearing ego. Self-consciousness involves the oddness of being able to talk to oneself, and with a disappearing sense of self, this capacity also weakens or disappears. When I speak to myself, it is I to myself, with the third self looking on and grasping it all. There is not just me, but also a double-me, and then a triple-me. Otherwise, the echo chamber of self-address would never happen. When the dementia of schizophrenia sets in, the me and the double-me are experienced by the third onlooker-me as mechanical speaking machines.[1] It is as if one's own thoughts are experienced as tape recorded conversations of someone else. Then, the third on looking me seems increasingly unreal and mechanical as well. Hence one's own thoughts or experience of oneself become wholly impersonal. It is the same as the complete vacuous nature of the inner world. Sometimes suicide is attempted as a response to the inward and unbearable hollowness experienced. It is an attempt to bring inward consistency to experience. The inner person is already dead. As a result, the destruction of the remaining outer shell, who is no longer really a person, brings coherence, since the revival

---

1. Zahavi, "Schizophrenia and Self-Awareness," 339–41.

or resuscitation of the inner person does not seem possible, and the outer "person" is an unbearable impersonal act.

Self-address, however, is not the ego's initial experience, nor is it sufficient to substantiate existence. One must first be addressed by others, and named by others. Typically, parents gift their children with the knowledge of themselves as persons. In a nightmare *Brave New World* scenario, a child hatched in a test tube and treated as a thing would probably never emerge to self-consciousness, and would probably not survive the test tube *in utero* period. We know that infants who are fed, clothed, and otherwise medically cared for, but never held or spoken to, suffer severe developmental damage.[2] The only people who can talk to themselves, and carry on a rich inner dialogue, are not the crazy, but the very sane who have had assurance and reassurance reiterated over many years that they are people with names and personalities.

Christian physician, Paul Tournier says:

> Perhaps the man on the street does not realize the gravity of this problem. The feeling that we exist seems so simple and natural to those of us who have been able to develop normally. Recently three of my patients told me, one after another, that they doubted their own existence. That means that they had the impression, almost impossible to express, of being automata or ghosts. They seemed to live, they acted, spoke, laughed, and cried, but always with the feeling that it was not really they who were doing so, but a being that was a stranger to themselves, or rather the appearance of a being.[3]

Tournier goes on to tell a remarkable story of one of these patients. The background of the case was very simple. When one of his patients was a young girl, her father punished her after a conflict. He pretended she did not exist for three days, and forbade anyone else to speak to her. Tournier writes, "What he did, in fact, was to destroy her consciousness that she existed." She grew up feeling herself to be a phantom, and was tormented with the doubt of her own reality.[4] What was a philosophical exercise for David Hume, was obviously a matter of the utmost seriousness for this simple woman. This is especially illuminating, because this woman was not a philosopher. She was a soul grappling existentially with the problem that

2. Harmon, "Physical Contact with Your Infant."

3. Tournier, *Place For You*, 104.

4. Ibid., 106.

modern thinkers have played with for centuries. Philosophers sometimes seem adolescent, and they play games that no adult would be so silly as to seriously engage in. However, a woman such as this does not seem adolescent at all. She has a serious problem.[5]

This woman's story demonstrates in extremity what is true in a more diluted way for far larger numbers of people. Most people do not directly doubt their own existence, but many find existence to be "thin" and unsubstantial. And while existence *per se* may not be in question, the principle datum of life for very large numbers of modern people is that life is empty, purposeless, and meaningless. In other words, life veers in the direction of nothingness. But if there is an answer for this great difficulty in its most extreme form, then there is also an answer for the problem in its lesser form.

In reference to another of these patients who or was found by a serious solution, Tournier writes:

> And yet such patients often themselves feel intuitively that their problem is a really a religious rather than a psychological one . . . . It was, however, following upon a religious experience that that patient was liberated from her doubts about her own existence. After dramatic interviews and exchanges of letters with the pastor she suddenly made a sort of Pascal's wager—"If God exists and I exist, I am willing to do whatever he asks!" An idea came into her mind, really rather an odd idea, but she obeyed it without hesitation. This reminds me of Christ's remark: "If any man's will is to do his will, he shall know whether the teaching is from God or whether I am speaking on my own authority" (John 7:17).[6]

This woman believed that God spoke to her, and she obeyed. Remarkably, that was the turning point. She began to know that she existed, for if God spoke to her, and she could respond, then she knew that she indeed, was "there." If she were a philosopher, her formulation, in opposition to Descartes would be more like, "God speaks, therefore I am." Or, more specifically, "God has spoken to me, therefore I am." This posits that a weak dependent personality is not ultimately dependent upon either itself, or upon other weak and dependent personalities for its existence and

---

5. I have personally known several people who seriously doubted their own existence. Pastors and counselors hear many things in confidence that the general public would find incredible.

6. Tournier, *Place For You*, 105.

sustenance, but finds its ultimate origin and identity in the Speaking God, specifically the God of the Bible.[7]

Here we come to a kind of *reductio ad absurdum*, or personalist cosmological argument. Every person is dependent upon prior persons to be a person. But where does this end or where does this begin? Is it conceivable that there is an infinite regress of finite persons to account for the reality of any given personality? What accounts for each prior personality that gives rise to the one following? Is prior personality sufficient to completely account for any personality at any given time? We have two choices, and, ultimately, *only* two. Either we owe our existence to ourselves (which carries within it some manifest impossibilities), or we owe our existence to God. Now my contention is quite simply that we, on a daily basis, are faced with the starkest contradiction imaginable. If we do not acknowledge the reality of the God of the Bible—if he does not exist—then neither do we. On the other hand, if we do exist, then he does too. Now the introduction of this stark contradiction may be a bit breathtaking and perhaps even shocking. But I would contend that our very existence brings us to this cliff, and to this very sharp either/or. In real life, however, it is ameliorated a bit by the recognition that if he does exist, and if we exist, but we refuse to acknowledge his existence, we don't go up in a puff of smoke and cease to be. Rather, the result (because of God's mercy and longsuffering with our foolishness) is both cognitive dissonance and existential confusion. Our existence will be at best "thin," and it will be incomprehensible. We will have no ground at all for our very being and personhood.

John Calvin opened his *Institutes of the Christian Religion* with this very beautiful paragraph:

> Our wisdom, in so far as it ought to be deemed true and solid Wisdom, consists almost entirely of two parts: the knowledge of God and of ourselves. But as these are connected together by many ties, it is not easy to determine which of the two precedes and gives birth to the other. For, in the first place, no man can survey himself without forthwith turning his thoughts towards the God in whom

---

7. This is a perfect modern illustration and application of chapter 18 of *The Westminster Confession*, which is on "Assurance": "This certainty is not a bare conjectural and probable persuasion grounded upon a fallible hope; but an infallible assurance of faith founded upon the divine truth of the promises of salvation, the inward evidence of those graces unto which these promises are made, the testimony of the Spirit of adoption witnessing with our spirits that we are the children of God, which Spirit is the earnest of our inheritance, whereby we are sealed to the day of redemption." Schaff, *Creeds of Christendom*, 3:638.

> he lives and moves; because it is perfectly obvious, that the endow-
> ments which we possess cannot possibly be from ourselves; nay,
> that our very being is nothing else than subsistence in God alone.
> In the second place, whose blessings, which unceasingly distil to
> us from heaven, are like streams conducting us to the fountain.[8]

Human consciousness necessarily involves consciousness of God. If the consciousness of God could be eradicated, then human self-consciousness would also disappear. Self-knowledge is possible only in God.

Of course, grant the premise of creation and a creator God, and every-thing I say follows. But why should I grant the premise? You should grant the premise because we either exist as a free creative act of this perfect God, and thus participate as created analogues in all of the real existent perfections of God, or we exist ultimately by chance, and partake in all of the analogues of that mistress. There is no third alternative. The analogues of God are (briefly) truth, goodness, and beauty. The analogues of chance are chaos, confusion, and disorder. Pure chance is perfectly unknowable. If you or I, or everything and anything, is the product of pure chance, this would be completely un-knowable, and the purely unknowable is no different from nothingness.

If you are driven mad by this conclusion this is exactly what the Bible itself would expect, and not a conclusion that the Bible would expect any man to take contentedly or serenely. The Bible (which is a long and difficult book) frankly diagnoses man, in his current state, as functioning every-where with this epistemological glitch. To be an unbeliever is the natural state of man, and to be otherwise is attributed to nothing short of a miracle. A man's unbelief is not simply neutral, or a state of being where one chooses to believe or not believe as one would choose a meal from a variegated menu. Unbelief occupies a religious position in a man's life, and is as deci-sive for the unbeliever as belief is for the believer.

There are two accounts of unbelief. The first account is that of the unbeliever himself. This is a necessary perspective, and it is not a simple, completely unified voice that speaks. Unbelief has as many voices as there are unbelievers. Not every voice is unique, though, and the absolute variety is not infinite. There are a certain number of objections to the Christian faith that cohere together, and not an uncountable number. Then, there is the diagnosis of the Bible itself concerning unbelief. The Bible has its own internal theology of unbelief and its own X-ray to offer. While the voice of the unbeliever itself ought to be heard, the most important voice is the

---

8. Calvin, "Institutes."

voice of the Bible. The reason the voice of the unbeliever needs to be heard is in order to demonstrate that the voice of unbelief is really the voice of caviling or of disputing with the judgment that God has already handed down in the court that he has called. This is what "doubt" is: *diakrinomoi*. The unbeliever is a "debater of this age" (1 Cor 1:20), and his unbelief is closely associated with bringing accusation and bringing charges of an ethical nature against God.[9] The doubter is, in fact, someone who himself calls God to account before his own bar of justice. The doubter is a judge who dares to question God, or dares to question that God, rather than he, ought to be the final judge. In other words, when we doubt God's existence and his governing power over all things, what we are really doing is ruling him out of court, and insisting that we have the final word. This brings us to all of the above contradictions and epistemologically reduces us to the necessity of self-existence, which is the same as nothingness. Undeniably, man almost compulsively wants to get on in life without this surrender and this necessary belief—man is ethically offended by this. Let me invite you to the next chapter, which examines man's penchant to always play the judge, even over God.

9. Barth, *Justification*, 67.

3

Ethics

IRONY IS BOTH REVEALING and concealing. It can also be very useful and especially effective when it is used as fire to fight fire. As we have seen, the Bible is replete with it. Biblical expressions of irony are often withering expressions of judgment on human "wind-baggery." Irony is meant to be funny, and it is funny at someone else's expense. Humor rests on a perceived incongruity that often is not perceived by the object of the joke in the first place. When it is perceived, it often will precipitate anger, because it has made that one an object of shame. Biblical irony and mockery are aimed at the self-inflation of very small people who imagine themselves to be very great. In a word, the Bible finds human conceit to be ridiculous, and God has a long, long laugh at the expense of the ridiculous.

The account given of the creation and subsequent fall of Adam and Eve in the book of Genesis shows the beginning of ethical selfism. Adam and Eve eat the forbidden fruit, and God refers to them as those who have come to know good and evil. What this means is that they now have fallen away from knowing the will of God, and of being able to obey it, and they have now, like God, become the authors of morality. They themselves will be the determiners of what is good and of what is evil. Their own selves become the source, and this is now thrust upon them. From that time forward, the creation of morality will be an onerous, and impossible, human burden. The modern world is now far more self-consciously "selfist" than the world was five minutes after the fall, and more so then it was in Jesus' own day. The seed of implication has been developing over time. And just as selfism leads to darkness in regard to the very possibility of self-knowledge or of any knowledge of the world, it also leads to darkness in regard to actions that are good, and actions that are bad. The assumption behind human ethics now is that the world and humanity are self-complete without reference to God, and this always leads to self-looping vicious circles in regard to human actions, because humanity is not self-complete, but now pretends that it is. We are saddled with this as a curse, but generally speaking, the human race understands it as its own highest glory.

In John 10, Jesus mocked his enemies by quoting a portion of Ps 82. This psalm uses a play on words that refers back again to Ps 115, 135, and to Isa 6. The psalm is a dressing down of unjust magistrates for not issuing just judgments that protect the weak and the needy from their oppressors. The psalm refers to these judges as "gods." This reference is a double entendre. Man as the image of God—particularly when he is invested with judicial powers as a judge—could be legitimately referred to as a "god." This is odd language for the Bible, because the Bible makes so much everywhere of the utter distinction between God and his creation, but not an impossible usage, because it is invested with a meaning that is different from paganism, and yet is playing in a double sense on paganism. Paganism inevitably allows for semi-divinity, or growing divinity on the part of men, or even animals. The Bible never permits this. The creation chapters of Genesis, at the very outset, make clear that the world, and the stars, and all that God created are not an expelling outward from his own inner essence. Creation is "out of nothing" or perhaps more properly, "into nothing." In pagan creation mythologies, the world is usually a refashioning by a god of some prior "stuff," or it is an excrescence of the god's own inner being. The entire world is potentially the stuff of "gods," or it is at least potentially divine. The Bible could legitimately refer to a man as a "god" in the sense that he may function analogously to God (as a judge for example), but it is an analogy of action, and never an identity of essence. In Ps 82, God mocks the judges of Israel for behaving just like pagan judges. They have no concern for justice. Beyond that, "they do not know, they do not understand, they walk about in darkness" (Ps 82:5). They should understand themselves to be, legitimately and honorably, gods under God. Instead, they have made themselves pagan gods, and now like the pagan idols, they cannot see, hear, or understand.

In John 10, Jesus is engaged in irony by quoting the Ps 82 to his enemies. Most of the chapter is about Jesus as the good shepherd, the true shepherd of Israel. This has long Old Testament roots, and contains within it an indictment of the religious leaders of Israel as bad shepherds. Portions of the Old Testament book of Ezekiel indict the pastors and shepherds of his day as self-absorbed exploiters and oppressors of the people, and promises are made that God will one day send a "good shepherd" who will bind up the wounds of the people and bring healing and health to them. Jesus claims to be this one. He is also, by implication, claiming that the shepherds of his day are the same as the shepherds of Ezekiel's day. In the midst of this discourse, he finally makes an open claim to being of one essence with the Father—"I and the Father are one"[1]—and it is then that the Jews want to stone him. Jesus asks for which good work are they going to stone him? They answer, not for any of his works, but for blasphemy. He quotes Ps 82 to them: "You are gods." If they, who only did evil works, were addressed as gods, why should not he, who did extraordinary, miraculous good works possible only to God, be accused of blasphemy? It is an argument from the lesser to the greater. If even those who are idolatrous can be referred to "gods" by God, then Jesus most certainly can be referred to reverently as the Son of God.

The irony of this is very deep, and the text reveals something most remarkable to us about the reality of the human condition. Mere human beings, who were created out of nothing, are now actually accusing God of blasphemy. This is rather backwards, and of course this accusation itself constitutes blasphemy on the part of the accusers. But the daring on the part of the Pharisees is breathtaking. Noah Webster's definition of blasphemy is as follows: "An indignity offered to God by words or writing; reproachful, contemptuous or irreverent words uttered impiously against Jehovah." Jesus offends the accusers because he dares to evaluate or judge them. They would accuse God of blasphemy for daring to question their supremacy and sovereign will. The result is a paradox: up is down, black is white, and good becomes evil. When the worship of the true God is abandoned and the self is embraced in a final sense, then ethical blindness is inevitable. Those who become gods themselves will "have neither knowledge nor understanding," and "they walk about in darkness" (Ps 82:5).

This brings us to an interesting turn. To repeat, the Bible indicates that inquiries into the existence of God are never neutral theoretical musings. They rather always have a particular ethical edge about them. They are interrogations, and have the character of accusation about them.[2] The deepest intention of questioning the existence of God is not ontological; rather, it is ethical. There is something prior to the question of existence, and the existence question is clouded. If I am god, and my determinations are final, then it is simply impossible for the God of the Bible to be God, or for Jesus to be God. The ethical accusation is that God is unjust, and has

1. John 10:30
2. Barth, *Justification*, 67.

no right to be God since this is now my office. If he exists, then his sheer existence is blasphemy. If he exists, then he is my enemy.[3] It is necessary either to mute his existence and remake him as less than the almighty God of the Bible, one who is smaller, who is satisfied to, at best, co-exist with me, or it is the case that he simply does not exist. If he does exist as the almighty God of the Bible, then this brings confusion and dissonance. If I cannot dismiss him, then I must accuse him. Dismissal is actually accusation, and in all likelihood there is a veering back and forth between the two. The mindset of fallenness is double-mindedness. In all cases, it is necessary to take things into one's own hands, and become one's own god determining good and evil for oneself.

Interestingly, God seems to take a step back and allow us to do just that. He says that he will give us a great privilege. He will allow us to create a law, and then he will judge us by that same law. Whatever judgments we bring to those around us will become the same standard of judgment that he will test us by. We have accused God of being an unjust judge. So God allows the privilege, and lets us determine our own standard. Hence, Aristotle will be judged by his own golden mean, Kant by his own categorical imperative, Sartre, who wanted to legislate for the entire world in his every decision, will be judged in the same way. In other words, it is a very dangerous thing to have the very power of determining both good and evil; it is fraught with terrible ironies. Jesus warned us about this in one of the most misused and misunderstood of all biblical texts, "Judge not, that ye be not judged" (Matt 7:1). The modern world quotes this often as a biblical justification for complete ethical tolerance, but it means exactly what it says. You will be judged as you judge, and we have now all had this burden inescapably thrust upon us.

If, for example, I am a very bad man, or a very selfish man, I ironically demand that everyone around me be completely altruistic in regard to me, and I am very angry if they are not. In the end, I will damn myself because I have so completely damned so many people around me for their lack of altruism toward me. If I am especially bold in my badness, I may even publicly say, "Every man for himself," and, "selfishness is the best policy." But my judgments of all of those around me who did not acknowledge the

3. In our current environment, the final, and supposedly unanswerable, defense against almost anything is the "I am offended" defense. This is subconsciously (and sometimes consciously) the great defense of the human race against the Living God— never mind that it is essentially without content.

supremacy of my needs and wants determines how I will be judged. I will be judged for my own lack of altruism that I demanded of everyone else.

If, however, I am a very "good" man, I am actually in a far more precarious position. The "good" cast their nets much further than the bad. The good have a penchant for legislating not just for themselves and their own wants, as does the selfish man, but for legislating for the entire world. Their demands may be not only severe, but also universal. It's important to note that fallen man told God, "I can run the world better than you." It is as if God says, "Then do so, and in the end we will test the results." Everyone knows the real results of "good" people who legislate for everyone else—it is tyranny. It is either petty tyranny in a family or work situation, or massive tyranny on the part of the great national and world tyrants. The blueprint for goodness that exists in the head, for some reason is never easily or without resentment accepted by those around. It is usually not even agreed upon by those around. More often than not, the judgments on others by the good are far more severe than the judgments of merely egotistical people. The irony is that all too easily, "goodness" becomes an elevated egotism that does not seek the satisfaction merely of the lower appetites and whims, but of pride. The ego demands to be the biggest and perhaps the only ego, and insists that it alone knows the formula for goodness. The real inner judgment towards those who will not submit is, "to hell with you for not doing as I say." But do you do as you say? If wrath and fury is the sentence carried out on anyone who would lie to cover ineptitude, for example, then so be it onto you when you lie for the same reason. By an odd psychological quirk, we are usually the angriest with our own faults seen in others. This reaches its peak of irony when the proud hate the proud for their pride.

There is a further step to this quandary. Even beyond being judged by our own standards, God has said that he will even permit us to judge *him*. As a race, we have declared him "out of court." We have determined that he is unjust. As we judge God, we too shall be judged, for we have declared that we are gods. "On that day when, according to my Gospel, God judges the secrets of men by Christ Jesus" (Rom 2:16). Jesus, who is the very word of God, was handed over to men to be judged. How will the world judge God when given the opportunity? Our judgment of him was self-damning. Here, the reality of the divine law connects with the reality/unreality of man's self-created law. On what basis of self-made law was Jesus crucified? Jesus was condemned because he claimed to be God, and because he claimed to be the true source of the judgment of good and evil.

This was called blasphemy, and for this he was put to death. If this same standard is brought against his accusers, what is the result? It can only be death, for each judge tacitly made exactly the same claim. If you claim that God deserves to die because he claims to be God, then you too deserve to die because you make the same claim.

The result is that every god will damn himself and every mouth will be stopped, and all secrets will be judged by Christ Jesus.

4

Can Saul Alinsky Be Saved?
(Or, Should Saul Alinsky Go To A.A.?)

> . . . And those whom he predestined he also called; and those
> whom he called, he also justified; and those whom he justified, he
> also glorified (Rom 8:30).

THE ABOVE PASSAGE IS a miniature, seed form in the Apostle Paul, of what
systematic theologians later developed into the *ordis salutis* ("the order of
salvation"). Without entering into the ins and outs of the *ordis*, it will suffice
to simply note that Paul does seem to be recounting some kind of logical,
and/or temporal progression of the work of redemption in individuals and
the church. For our purposes, I would like to do something a little different
with the passage, and loosely apply it to the progression of history.

Every era applies the whole of the Bible to the whole of life. However
badly, or inadequately, there is no doctrine, no portion of the Bible that is
not to some degree present and active in both the church and the world,
precisely because this is ultimately the work of the Holy Spirit. However, it
is also the case that every era, by necessity, magnifies some portion of the
Bible to fit the particular crisis or need of that time. In very short order, let
me attempt an historical application, and in this, we can see the gradual
creation of the modern self. We can see where the modern self came from,
and how we got to where we are. The modern self is inconceivable apart
from the work of the gospel, and our response and reaction to it.

PREDESTINED

We are accustomed to associating predestination with John Calvin's Reformation, and this is not untrue. However, the really revolutionary grasp and

application of predestination was not enacted at the time of the Reformation (which was a re-remembering and re-application), but more than a thousand years before by Augustine of Hippo. By all accounts, St. Augustine was one of the greatest minds in the history of the world, and one church's greatest theologians. He applied this doctrine in the midst of the collapsing Roman Empire. C. N. Cochrane's masterful *Christianity and Classical Culture* outlines the paradoxical consequences of predestination on this era.[1]

The collapsing Roman Empire was transfixed with a feeling and a belief in *fate*. The caste system of Hinduism has a paralyzing effect on all who are born into it and continue to believe in it. If one is born into a begging caste, for example, one is fated from past lives to be a beggar—nothing else is possible. It is not just far eastern Hinduism that is riddled with the consequences of fate. Fate is a fairly common doctrine and belief in all of paganism; the Romans were no exception. If one adds to an underlying belief in fate on the part of all ancients, the accelerating decline and coming collapse of Rome, fate in the form of astrology, became a paralyzing influence. Similar to the way that a Hindu birth determines their caste, the configurations of stars and planets determined the fate of a newborn Roman.

In what may be counterintuitive, Augustine's biblical application of predestination freed the Christian of that era from the deadly sense of being fated. Predestination was the fountainhead of freedom and the possibility of responsible action. "If God be for me, who can be against me" is a very cheerful Christian sentiment authored by Paul, and echoed by all of his readers since he penned those words. God, and all of his infinite power is *for* me and has determined that through thick or thin, I will be remade in the image of Jesus Christ. Jesus Christ is the one true man, who has entered history, and is the only human ever to have escaped all of the determinants of "the principalities and powers, the world rulers of this present age" (Eph 6:12). Jesus Christ is the one truly free man, who was free to serve God with no hindrance of sinful shadow. If I am predestined to be made over in the image of Jesus, I am paradoxically predestined to be free. Augustinian predestination was predestination to freedom. This was revolutionary in the midst of the depressing determinism and fatalism of collapsing Rome. It remade the world, and gave fresh confidence to a failing human race.

---

1. Cochrane, 456–516.

CALLED

With the collapse of Rome, monastic communities developed everywhere. The monastic communities were remarkably vital, and carried within themselves all of the life of the gospel in a ruined world. The monks became the missionaries. The monks increasingly moved northward to the wild and uncivilized tribal peoples. They built manor houses, cleared the forests, farmed the land, and chanted the psalms as spiritual warfare. Gradually, they converted the barbarians who often martyred and slaughtered them. But as *the predestined ones*, over time, they converted and spiritually conquered their barbarian and tribal enemies. The tribes were called by God through the monkish missionaries. This is one of the greatest triumphs in the history of the world. This missionary movement laid the groundwork of what came to be known as Europe, and that great civilization would have been impossible without it.

Tribal life is very deep, but conversely, just as narrow. Tribes move constantly, and are primarily warrior peoples, living by constant warfare. Many tribal names mean, "the people." Tribal peoples typically regard their own tribe as the *only* fully human people. Those outside of the tribe are fit for little except enslavement, death, or rape. While tribal confederations do exist, they are fragile and the exception.

When the monks were *called*, they were called by one God and Father, one Lord Jesus Christ. If each tribe were called by the same God, then the totem of each tribe with its various gods and ancestors overlooking the tribe and its unchanging tribal customs was replaced by one and the same God. Each tribe now worshipped the same God, and this God had one law for all tribes. The law is the revelation and fulfillment of love, according to Paul (Rom 13:8-10). The tribes were now called to love one another instead of annihilate one another in constant internecine warfare.

All of the tribes now also had one great chief in Jesus Christ, and blood thirst (perhaps the prime passion and motive behind all tribal life)[2] was now slaked in each and all tribes by eating his body and drinking his blood.

---

2. Goldman, *End of the World*, 89. Goldman writes, "Two billion war deaths would have occurred in the twentieth century if modern societies suffered the same casualty rate as did primitive peoples, according to anthropologists Lawrence H. Keeley. He has calculated that two thirds of primitives were at war continuously, typically losing half a percent of their population to war each year."

JUSTIFIED

Theologians have typically identified three offices of the law.[3] The first office of the law is to teach us what is good, and what the will of God is for each of us. The second office is to teach us what is "civic righteousness," that is, what ought the state to require as lawful and unlawful. And the third office is to teach us that we are sinners. It is, bluntly, to condemn us, and to turn us over to the power of death in our flesh as those who are incapable of keeping the law perfectly, or, for that matter, even adequately. The monks preached the gospel to the tribes using the first office of the law. The law of God was a better way of life. It taught them that even though he belongs to the bear tribe, and she belongs to the wolf tribe, they have the same God and the same chief in Jesus Christ. It taught them that it was unlawful to steal their life either in murder or in slavery. It taught them that they were obligated to respect each other's property, to value their lives, to honor them with the truth, and to covet nothing that their one God has seen fit to give to them. Even if such commandments were hard, or impossible for them to keep on their own, by the power given them by their common father, our common chief, and the Holy Spirit, they could begin to be new men and women, and in real measure keep this law. This is the gospel of law preached by Paul in Rom 13:8–10. It is the gospel of love. The tribes began to love one another, and to have common kings, which were slowly transformed into kingdoms that we would now begin to recognize as the outlines of the nations of Europe.

After a few hundred years of this kind of gospel, however, he who was being transformed into the European Christian man began to be more and more aware of his sinfulness, his imperfections, his incapability. He became increasingly aware of the demand of God and of the demand of God's law for perfection. A dizzyingly complex sacramental system was developed by the church to deal with the Christian's sinfulness. The church had developed what amounted to a Ptolemical system of sacraments with increasing cycles within cycles, and epicycles within epicycles to cover this growing awareness of sinfulness. In the midst of this, a great theological Galileo was raised up, who, in a great theological and biblical intuition, transformed our understanding of the starry heavens, and placed a new sun at the center of our galaxy, which produced a stunning new simplicity and order. Martin

3. This would be Mosaic Law, of which the center would be the Ten Commandments (Exod 20:1–17; Deut 5:1–21).

Luther, who was, in his own soul, a complete transcription of all that was wrong with his own Christian age, grasped justification by faith. This was the new sun at the center, and it transformed epicycles within epicycles and brought forgiveness of sin through justification squarely to the center. Guilt-ridden European man was now transformed into forgiven Christian man, and he found a glorious new liberty.

GLORIFIED

We have now reached the end of Paul's *ordo*, and we have reached our own time. Paul tells us the final stage—after being justified—is to be glorified, and notice, it is translated in the past tense. I emphasize this because we are accustomed to thinking of glorification as something that happens after we die and are resurrected. That may well be true in its fullness, but Paul clearly believes there is a present application in this life.

Paul elsewhere says, "And we all, with unveiled face, beholding the glory of the Lord, are being changed into his likeness from one degree of glory to another" (2 Cor 3:18). We find this littered throughout the New Testament. In John 17, in Jesus' high priest prayer, he says this: "Father, I desire that they also, whom thou hast give me, may be with me where I am, to behold my glory which thou hast given me before the foundation of the world" (John 17:24). It is clear that the final completion of this is in the Resurrection, but it has a fulfillment now as we behold him by faith, as Paul stated above. Jesus further says, "The glory which thou hast given me, I have given them" (John 17:22).

We have reached our own, de-glorified and denuded era. Our era is not spoken to in its initial need (as a "felt need") by any of what has previously broken in. While every renewal from all times past are necessary for our time, our time demonstrably has its own unique need as the triumph of Christ in history moves forward and moves deeper to elements that still have not been renewed and overcome.

DE-GLORIFICATION

I have now suggested that the peculiar crisis of our time is what I have termed our lack of glory. Let me go further and suggest that it is more than that—we have been "de-glorified." The reason we have been de-glorified *ultimately* is because the effect of the Gospel is always to empty the world before the world is refilled with Gospel renewal. The world always has its own idolatrous version, a version that is filled out in the current "world rulers," the "principalities and powers" that control that era. Eras before us have been far more glorious, in spite of the particular glories of our own age. However, there are penultimate causes that show us how we got here.

The first penultimate cause that I would raise is that we are too far removed from our own tribal heritage. The glow, the light, of the great warrior, is too far from us. It is so far removed from us that we can no longer remember if we are of white European extraction, that our heritage is as tribal as the Apache, Sioux, or Cherokee. The Vandals, the Goths, the Vikings, the Gauls, and a thousand other peoples were tribal. Tribes live and die by glory and honor. They are not ethical cultures; they are honor cultures. That sense of honor and glory is finally gone. It extended and maintained itself for a long, long time in the Western world and in the great monarchies of Europe, but the monarchies were finally either eliminated, or contained, so even in remaining ones—such as the British monarchy—they no longer really exercise power, and are nearly reduced to garnishes and decoration. The British are very ambivalent about their own monarchy.[4] On the one hand, they consider it an eternal and indispensable institution, and on the other, consider it outworn and useless. The monarchy is certainly premodern and an anachronism; it is both charming and barren.

Secondly, the Enlightenment initiated the final de-glorification of the West. And again, if viewed in a large enough venue, the Enlightenment was the servant of Christ. All glory in this world has been despoiled in order to make new room for the glory of Christ.

In 1992, Francis Fukuyama published a book length meditation on the de-glorification of our age entitled *The End of History and the Last Man*.[5] The book is a meditation on the philosophical enquiries of Friedrich Hegel and Friedrich Nietzsche. Fukuyama believed that we had reached the last stage of history, a kind of "end of history," in the triumph of democratic capitalism. Democratic capitalism, he believed, was stable, peaceful, and boring. It was achieved only by Nietzsche's "last man," who is a de-glorified "shop keeper," a man of commerce, a man with "no chest."[6] He is the man who has had all the glorious, heroic, warrior elements excised from his being.

4. Muggeridge, "Does England," 3–11.

5. Fukuyama, *End of History*.

6. Lewis, *Abolition of Man*, 35.

Let me briefly summarize Fukuyama's philosophy. Enlightenment philosophers woke up to find rotten monarchies and kings all around them. As have all royalty and aristocrats through history, these kings were fueled by glory. The glory of the late French court before the French Revolution is difficult for us to grasp. A king was vested with luminosity, splendor, and pomp that are quite foreign to the modern outlook. Those around him were able to bask in that glory, whether they were aristocrats or commoners. Aristocrats most commonly sought glory in war. Despite the influence of Christianity in creating and transforming Europe, the European society was in many ways still reminiscent of the world of Homer. The king and the aristocrat were primarily motivated by what the Greeks called *thymos*, which is root word for "heat." It means "glory seeking," and it was, in large part, satisfied in battle. A good reading of the *Iliad* and an understanding of the heroes of the Trojan War—Agamemnon, Hector, the Ajaxes, Ulysses, Achilles, and Patroclus—will thoroughly introduce any reader to what is comprehensively meant by *thymos*.[7] Europe was riddled by war—constant, civilization-destroying, glory-seeking war. The partial narrative for most Straussians[8] is that the great project of the Enlightenment philosophers was to cut the *thymotic* part of the soul out of man, and replace it with the acquisitive part. Man was to become a producer and consumer. In other words, he was to become a capitalist, or a wage earner working for the capitalist.

The great advantage of this theory is that energies—which previously might have gone into warfare, plunder, glory-seeking anger, and the seeking of honor through battle—will now be transformed into wealth production. The great satire of this type of man is Dickens' Ebenezer Scrooge. Scrooge may be an unpleasant sort, but he is not busy with war. In spite of his own personal spleen and ungraciousness toward the poor, Scrooge is a wealth producer who actually does more to eradicate poverty and beggary than all charitable activities that ever have been before him.[9] Adam Smith did not

7. Plato comprehensively examines "thymos" in Book 4 of *The Republic*.

8. These are disciples of the great University of Chicago political philosopher, Leo Strauss. Amongst them are both Fukuyama and Allan Bloom, who wrote *The Closing of the American Mind*. New York: Simon and Schuster, 1987.

9. Berkeley, "Towards the End of Poverty." This article asserts that capitalism is responsible for the greatest reduction of poverty in history in the late twentieth and early twenty-first centuries. Berkeley writes, "The world's achievement in the field of poverty reduction is, by almost any measure impressive. Although many of the original MDGs (Millennium Development Goals)—such as cutting maternal mortality by three-quarters and child mortality by two-thirds—will not be met, the aim of halving global poverty between 1990 and 2015 was achieved five years early . . . The MDGs may have helped

trust in Christian virtue to produce social cooperation and unselfish action; rather, Smith proposed that unselfishness and mutually beneficial actions would be produced through the miracle of "enlightened self-interest."[10]

Scrooge is a secular monk. His dress is as drab as a monk, and he is not given to frivolity of any sort.[11] He works, and he expects those around him to work. A gentleman, an aristocrat, a king, all delight in frivolity and useless things; they can only acquire the wealth necessary for such activities in plunder of other's wealth.

Democratic capitalist nations do not go to war with one another (or, at least, that is the theory) because in doing so, they would go to war with one's own market. If the ideal of international capitalism is achieved, it is thinkable that war will be abolished. Even now, it is surely true that what puts a check on Red China's martial aspirations is the fact that China is, to a large degree, being transformed into a capitalist producer and consumer nation, even if the democratic part has not yet jelled.

The Enlightenment has succeeded, but it has succeeded at the expense of glory. Can man live without glory? As Allan Bloom has observed, in these sorts of regimes, the citizen at least slightly despises himself. Self-esteem is a crisis, and the ego is weakened. No aristocrat suffers from this lack of self-esteem.[12]

However, there is another element in the Enlightenment itself that has led to our de-glorification—the Enlightenment has left us naked.

Much of the Enlightenment project was to "see through" everything. It was, in large measure, a movement aimed at the church and the church's control of much, if not most, of the social order. In order to achieve this aim, it became necessary to attack the veracity of the Christian faith. This is not the place to examine those arguments but merely to notice them. The Enlightenment was as vigorous an assertion of the autonomy of man as had yet appeared in Western thought. One of the cornerstones and effects of this sometimes violent assertion was reductionism. This was the beginning of the reduction of everything, including man himself to "nothing but . . ."

---

marginally, by creating a yardstick for measuring progress, and by focusing minds on the evil of poverty. Most of the credit, however, must go to capitalism and free trade, for they enable economies to grow—and it was growth, principally, that has eased destitution."

10. There is also a higher view of capitalism, which George Gilder has magnificently developed. In Gilder's view, capitalism can be and should be the Christian view and, on this basis, abounds in glory. Gilder, *Wealth and Poverty*.

11. Real monks, of course, are notoriously given to frivolity, playfulness, and joy.

12. Bloom, *Closing of the American Mind*, 250.

Man is no longer the image of God, but nothing but, and that is eventually reduced to, along with all other things, matter in motion. Darwinism eventually provided what, to the Enlightenment world, is a credible creation account that gave rationalization to the staggering complexity of life.

If the project of the Enlightenment was to "see through" everything, then this is the same as being naked, and as everybody knows, nakedness is the source of shame. A man in his nakedness is ashamed, and has no glory.

THE TWO TREES

Let us now revert to what has already been somewhat repetitively examined: the biblical account of the fall. In previous chapters, we have indeed examined the consequences of the fall into sin extensively. But now we want to deepen our analysis and examine a "what if" question. We know a great deal about what actually *did* happen as a result of disobeying God (and *that*, we have examined) but now in our deepened analysis, we will examine more about what *ought* to have happened, and beyond that, the consequences that have ensued as a result of the church *not* adequately pursuing this line of thought. All of this impinges a great deal on the modern deficit of glory.

In Gen 3, we see a continuation of the story of Gen 2. Before the creation of Eve, Adam is alone in the garden of Eden, not having a "suitable helpmeet." Before Eve's creation, God has explained to Adam that he may eat of every tree of the garden, save one. He is not to eat of the Tree of the Knowledge of Good and Evil, but of every other tree (including The Tree of Life) he is to eat.[13] Later, after Adam has named the animals, and become aware of his lack of a suitable helpmeet, he is put to sleep by God. God takes a rib from Adam's body and creates from it Eve. Upon awakening, and seeing her, we have the world's first love poem. "This at last is bone of my bones and flesh of my flesh; she shall be called woman (*ishasha*) because she was taken out of the man (*ish*)" (Gen 2:23).

The serpent, which was craftier, or subtler than any other beast in the field, tempted them, and Eve partook of the forbidden fruit. She offered some to her husband, and he, too, ate. For this crime, they are cast out of the garden, and cursed with death.

For our purposes, it is significant that Adam and Eve are forbidden by God to partake of a fruit that will enable them "to be like God." The

13. A literal translation of the Hebrew is "eat,eat," translated "freely eat," in the NKJV, or "surely eat," in the NIV.

"knowledge of good and evil"—or, a significant capacity for moral discernment—is precisely what enables them to "be like God." God does not want them to have this. Children of the Enlightenment made much of God withholding permission for this knowledge.

John Milton produced his epic masterpiece, *Paradise Lost,* in 1667. By the nineteenth century, the Romantic critics were saying very significant things about Milton's re-telling of the creation and fall account. Beginning with William Blake, and continuing with Percy Shelley, a line of criticism was produced that became the standard Romantic line. In effect, it retells the story through the eyes of the Enlightenment.

Blake, Shelley, and others began a line of literary criticism, which claimed that Satan was actually the secret hero of the poem; even further, they claimed that this was Milton's intention all along. Satan, they maintained, was by far the most interesting figure in the poem. Satan was actually a kind of liberator. Adam and Eve, even in the garden, were in thralldom to a tyrant, and a boring tyrant at that. Jehovah wanted and intended for Adam and Eve to only be obedient ciphers, unquestioning children, and unthinking parrots. God did not want adults who were capable of thinking on their own. He wanted children—eternal, obedient, and unquestioning children.

This line of thought has strongly influenced a whole line of leftist social theorists, including Karl Marx. In recent years, it has found its way into the American mainstream through Saul Alinsky, who was mentor and teacher to both Secretary Hillary Clinton and President Barack Obama. In what amounts to a theological premise to an entire way of thinking, acting, and being, that is wholly in concert with the Romantic critics, although, probably not recognized as such, we find this as a dedication on the fly page of Alinsky's famous *Rules for Radicals:*

> Lest we forget at least an over-the-shoulder acknowledgment to the very first radical: from all our legends, mythology, and history (and who knows where mythology leaves off and history begins— or which is which), the first radical known to man who rebelled against the establishment and did it so effectively that he at least won his own kingdom—Lucifer.[14]

The fall, according to the Milton critics, was a fall upward, a fall up to maturity and true humanity. The heart and essence of man is to be found in rebellion against authority.

14. Alinsky, *Rules for Radicals.*

Authority is oppressive, by definition. Initially, authority was found through the church. However, as things have developed, we see it take the form more generically as simple authority. For Marx, it was the oppressive authority of the capitalist over the proletariat. In the 1960s it was the authority of the Establishment, in whatever form it took. It was into this time and atmosphere that Alinsky wrote *Rules for Radicals*.

The question as to whether humanity was meant to come to the knowledge of good and evil had there not been a fall is an unsettled question in the history of dogma. I suggest that the inadequacy and incompleteness of our answer to this question has been ultimately pernicious.

The church has been ambiguous, and perhaps ambivalent in its exegesis of the second and third chapters of Genesis. Is it true that God did not want Adam and Eve, and their progeny, to ever know and participate in the knowledge of good and evil? Indeed, is it not doubtful that real humanity could ever exist apart from moral discernment? And what kind of God would want to keep us from such knowledge? Is he indeed, such a small and envious God that he begrudges us such knowledge?

Traditionally, it has always been asserted that the fall was catastrophic. But what if Adam and Eve had remained faithful to God's original commandment to eat of one tree but abstain from the other? Was the human race ever intended to have, in any form, the knowledge of "good and evil," or does the original prohibition against eating from that tree tell us that it was always and only a forbidden temptation? Was it an evil tree?

Almost universally, the Western Church's stand is ambivalent on the question. If the fruit had not been eaten, would this knowledge have *ever* been human knowledge, and if not, would it ever have been missed? Would "sinlessness" have always implied ignorance, and a non-participation in a knowledge that was "like God's?"[15] Most commentators concentrate on Adam and Eve's disobedience of the explicit commandment from God to not eat of the fruit of the Tree of the Knowledge of Good and Evil, and on the consequences for the human race, but drop the issue at that. They leave dangle the question of what was meant to be. John Calvin, for example, never even raises the "what if" question. Neither do Luther nor Augustine.

Dietrich Bonhoeffer brilliantly writes, in the very first pages of *Ethics*, many of the consequences of the fall into sin (and we have followed him

---

15. We immediately encounter a problem here. The ability to obey or disobey the prohibition against eating is already an act of moral discernment, albeit the act of a minor and not an adult.

in much of his analysis). Bonhoeffer shows, for example, how the fall led to the fall away from our one true Origin, and how Adam became his own source and origin. Subsequently, all of Adam's actions now issue from the loss of unity and the splitness in his person. Fallen and sinful man is a divided man—a man in conflict—and the original unity of the world and of human action has been lost. The very existence of ethics is itself a proof of the fall into sin. Bonhoeffer says that the very first task of a Christian ethic is to obviate ethics in the first place.[16] A culminating example would be the Scribes and the Pharisees, in the gospels, whom he terms "men of conscience."

> "For the Pharisee every moment of life becomes a situation of conflict in which he has to choose between good and evil. For the sake of avoiding any lapse his entire thought is strenuously devoted night and day to the anticipation of the whole immense range of possible conflicts, to the reaching of a decision in these conflicts, and to the determination of his own choice."[17]

Bonhoeffer emphasizes that when Jesus comes into contact with the Pharisees, they can do nothing else than attempt to draw him into their own conflicts and test him with them. Conscience is itself already the sign of the divided soul. The knowledge of good and evil is treated in an entirely negative way, and in this, we want to move beyond Bonhoeffer. In *The Pentateuch*, Keil and Delitzsch struggle with the question of the knowledge of good and evil as well; however, they never address the discomfort they feel with entire success. Keil and Delitzsch affirm that Adam and Eve would eventually have come to this knowledge, but only through perseverance in obedience to the prohibition, and through never partaking of that fruit. In some way, humanity would then have grown into this knowledge, but they strike an uncertain note, here; the knowledge of good and evil is exactly what was forbidden, and they believe the tree would have remained forever beyond bounds.[18]

There is, however, another possible answer: the Tree of Knowledge was to be forbidden only temporarily.[19] This is a simple solution. Many things are not innately wrong or bad, but are a matter of timing, and if

16. Bonhoeffer, *Ethics*, 17–20.

17. Ibid., 27.

18. Keil and Delitzsch, *Pentateuch*, 1:91–108.

19. This answer was propounded by some of the Eastern Fathers, but the one person I know of who has most significantly and thoroughly proposed it is James Jordan, an Old Testament scholar. Jordan, "Rebellion," 38–80; Jordan, "Dominion Trap."

partaken of too soon, can lead to death in either a literal or metaphorical sense. We can ask certain simple questions to make the point. "Is sex wrong?" No, but someone wanting sex at age twelve is committing folly, and is actively killing his or her future ability to enter into marriage in a healthy way. Or, for example, let's imagine my eight-year-old son comes to me and says, "Can I have the keys to the car?" There is nothing wrong with driving a car, but unless I am highly irresponsible or do not care about my child's life, I will not allow him to drive the car. In eight or nine years, the request is not necessarily a bad request, but now is too soon.

Likewise, biblically, the desire to see God is not evil, but in this world, it is too soon. Here we know God primarily by means of the ear. The beatific vision is reserved for the hereafter, and trying to fulfill that desire now leads straight to idolatry. Similarly, it was not wrong for Israel to want a king. The law made just such a provision (Deut 17:14–20), but Israel sinned in wanting a king too soon in the case of Gideon, and of Saul, and for that matter, of Jesus who could only be enthroned following his resurrection (John 6:15).

Is it just possible that the second tree, the Tree of the Knowledge of Good and Evil, was to be eaten? Was it to be eaten after a lapse of probationary time during which they matured? Indeed, much later, when Solomon had become a king, he was asked in a dream by God what he wanted; Solomon's answer was that he wanted the capacity to discern between good and evil in order to be able to rule the people of Israel justly (I Kings 3:9). Interestingly, God did not rebuke Solomon, and tell him he was replicating the sin of his forefather, Adam. Indeed, he was commended for the request and rewarded for it.

Further on in the New Testament, we are told the very mark of the desired maturity in a Christian, is the capacity to distinguish good from evil (Heb 5:11–14). In a hint that we are on the right track with our interpretation, the writer of the letter to the Hebrews tells us that "*babes* need milk, and are unskilled in the word of righteousness," but that "solid food belongs to those who are of full age, which is those who by reason of use have their senses exercised to *discern both good and evil.*"[20] Perhaps Adam and Eve were moral "babes?"

---

20. Italics are included by me for emphasis.

THE EUCHARIST

The Lord's Supper or the Eucharist are, on some level, a replay every week, of what ought to have happened in the garden of Eden. Clearly, something is added, because the Eucharist is also a replay of the death of Christ, which is reenacted in the light of his resurrection. I am implying that Adam and Eve, if they had partaken of the Tree of Knowledge in an appropriate way, would have also experienced some kind of death. What initially was a threat would have been transformed into a promise.

Adam and Eve almost immediately partook of the Tree of the Knowledge of Good and Evil. Let me suggest that this corresponds to the cup of wine. The cup of wine is blood; it is death. The shedding of blood is the ultimate calling of a king. Solomon was called to be a king, and his first acts were acts of execution (1 Kgs 2). Adam and Eve were still moral children, not yet called to rule, but still in the apprenticeship of obedience. That is why it was proper for Solomon to request the ability to "distinguish good from evil." He must rule, he must critique, he must judge, he must finally even pass sentence, even if that sentence means death. The knowledge of good and evil is serious stuff. It is the stuff of what adults may be called to do and may have to do. It is to act like God himself as vice regent or under lord under him. At some point, Adam may have been called to execute justice on the serpent. This could only have happened *after* God had given permission to eat of the Tree of Knowledge.[21]

We always partake of the cup *after* we have partaken of the bread—never before. To reverse the order is not arbitrary. To reverse the order is to replay the fall in the Garden, because the cup represents the Tree of the Knowledge of Good and Evil.

The bread, which is the Body of Christ, also corresponds to the first tree—The Tree of Life. The first tree represents pure reception and gratitude for it. What do we have that we have not received? It represents gratitude for that reception; it represents joy. And lastly, as the crown, it is the Tree of

---

21. It is still possible this would have entailed some kind of death. Jordan distinguishes between "good death," and "bad death." Adam had already experienced one kind of death when God caused a "deep sleep" to come upon him when he removed a rib and created Eve. This was already a kind of death and resurrection that did not involve the "bad death" following sin. "Good death" would have entailed a kind of ascension or graduation from one degree of glory to another. The death of Christ has brought this result while "absorbing" "bad death" in atonement. Jesus re-opened the way for "good death." We still move from "one degree of glory to another" even after the sting of sin and "bad" death have been removed for us by Christ. Jordan, "Dominion Trap."

Play. It represents the proper occupation of children. Children are meant to be about the serious occupation of play.

Play is life without consequence, and this is necessary as the foundation for learning the things that adults will do. When little girls play "nurse" and "mommy" with their dolls, they are learning the serious business of being a mother or a nurse. They cannot properly learn without this play. When little boys play "cops and robbers," "soldier" or "cowboys and Indians," they are learning the serious occupation of being a protector and avenger of injustice. One cannot learn these things without first playing these serious offices without consequence and in complete safety. All of these occupations are "fun." Nothing is more important to the execution of serious adult offices than first being receptive, being grateful and thankful, being joyful, playing and having fun.

If one reverses these offices, then one immediately becomes a judge, a ruler, a critic, even an executor, and one does this in the awful state of childhood. Robespierre and Marie Antoinette unwittingly become our role models.[22]

To paraphrase Jacques Maritain in his quip about Kantianism, one does a critique of knowledge before anything is known. Or to paraphrase C. S. Lewis in his depiction of the current state of the West, when one has seen through everything, there is nothing left to see.[23] The child critic knows nothing; he has received nothing. He becomes a carping critic before he has ever been joyful. He has worked before he has played. He is by definition ungrateful because before he is grateful for having received, he has already "seen through." He is not a competent judge; he is a cynic, a nihilist. To be blunt, he is something of a brat. He is naked, and as a result, he is ashamed. The first thing this child critic sees through is his own self, yet he despises himself, and understands that he is "nothing but" dust.

One of the great difficulties that theorists and practitioners are up against—from Blake, Shelley, and Byron to Alinsky—is what happens if their protagonists win? From Robespierre through Lenin to our current time, this becomes an insoluble dilemma. They now *become* the new Establishment. They have no doctrine of authority that does not see authority as oppressive and inherently evil. The only solution to this dilemma is to

---

22. That is, the mythical Marie Antoinette who supposedly said of the starving peasants who had no bread, "Then, let them eat cake . . ." The real Marie Antoinette was kindly, pious, and was a cruelly treated victim of the revolutionary mob, which ended in a horrible and unjust execution.

23. Lewis, *Abolition of Man,* 91; Maritain, *Distinguish or Unite,* 74.

promote "eternal revolution," endless chaos and endless opposition. That culture will masochistically undermine and destroy itself in orgies of self-hatred and self-contempt.[24] Eventually, one reaches an inevitable point where chaos can only be completely destructive and nothing is left to rule. One reaches for the final possibility, which is simply to become an oppressive tyrant. Modern history is littered with terrible examples.

A simple illustration of the consequence of romantic rebellion can be seen now all over the western world in the "compulsive and addictive" personality. The great discovery of Alcoholics Anonymous was that the very center of addiction is to be found in rebellion.[25] Every young Byronic hero, every young James Dean, imagines himself a hero even if he does not have a cause, or *especially* if he is without a cause. The essence of this young hero is that he is "in charge" and answerable to no one. Ironically, the effect of a life in which "no one will tell me what to do," is that one loses control at the most basic levels. One becomes not a freed man, but a slave, even to the most basic of bodily appetites. Sex, alcohol, drugs, food, and potentially a thousand substances or behaviors become the rulers and kings of the will. The will loses executive authority. The cure for the will to regain its own authority and effectiveness is, ironically, in surrender. One confesses powerlessness ("Hi, my name is Joe, and I am an alcoholic") and one surrenders ("My life is out of control and can only be restored to sanity by a Higher Power"). The "Twelve Steps" are essentially a statement of what the Bible calls repentance.[26] In this case, the alcoholic must first become a grateful

24. One sees this with peculiar clarity in American, British, and Western European universities. Though they began as Christian institutions, their authorities have been compelled to hate and destroy themselves by their almost universally embraced Leftism. Our great universities are the New Establishments, and they all writhe in contorted self-hatred. The only way to cope with so much contradiction is by donning the cape of hypocrisy. What began in the gospels with the scribes and the Pharisees is now cultural *carte blanche* in our ongoing cultural encounter with Jesus. Tom Wolfe became the great chronicler of these phenomena, which he came to term "Radical Chic." So-called liberal guilt is the same phenomena more broadly applied. See Wolfe, "Radical Chic."

25. The Latin word "addictus" from which we derive the English word, "addiction," is a suitable Latin translation for the Greek word, "paradokin" which is found three times in Rom 1:24, 26, 28 and can be translated "to be given over." The consequence for rebellion against God, is "to be given over" uncontrollably, to base character and behavior. "Addiction" is to be "given over" by God because of rebellion against him. This simple word study tells us a lot about our current culture.

26. One of the most common objections to A.A. is that it says that alcoholism is a "disease." Surely this is "straining at a gnat." Even Thomas Szasz, who wrote a devastating book called *The Myth of Mental Illness*, acknowledges that "illness" can be used as a figure

child again. It is only by reliving a proper childhood and then re-doing much of what has been one in pre-mature and perverse adulthood, that he can then enter mature adulthood with adult self-control. He will then be able to exercise adult executive authority.

> He (the alcoholic) is a maladjusted, immature individual who has developed few techniques for alleviating his feelings of discomfort. Actually his attitude implies that he will not recognize limitations or inadequacies in his personality, will not admit them. In order to convince himself that he has no need to compromise or inhibit his reactions, he deliberately exposes himself to irritating and challenging stimuli instead of insulating himself against them. There is a certain 'grandiosity' a certain omnipotence in such behavior. This refusal to accept his personality problems in a way that would enable him to work with them and build up the more acceptable forms of compensation is one of the most striking characteristics of the alcoholic personality as revealed in the Rorschach test protocols. If he cannot accept the idea of limitation and inadequacy, the conflict must be outside himself, and he proceeds to externalize it.[27]

Let me suggest that this tells us, on a small and particular scale, what is true on a much larger and more general scale. The culture that bases itself on rebellion against revelation will not find the liberty and freedom that it imagines, but rather it will only find enslavement to what is low and base.

If the above answer is correct, then the ambiguities of the doctrine of the two trees are resolved and the "pernicious doctrine" is avoided. The calling of the human race was not to remain eternal and unquestioning children, but they were, indeed from the beginning, meant to grow up into rulers who judged between good and evil. Adam and Eve were meant to "graduate" to the second tree.

---

of speech in a legitimate way. Even beyond Szasz, Jesus described himself as "physician" who came to call the "sick." Nobody complains that Jesus, apparently centuries ahead of his time, mistakenly incorporated a "medical model" in reference to all of the unpleasantries around publicans and tax collectors. It is an ironic complaint because, while A.A. does say that alcoholism is a "disease," they proceed to deal with it, with remarkable incisiveness, as a sin (incisiveness that more often than not puts the church to shame). The old Oxford Group, which was the parent group of A.A., often referred to people as being "sin sick," an apt metaphor, and surely what A.A. means in using the term "disease." Initially, A.A. was a comprehensively Christian group, and only later was its Christian character weakened. Szasz, *Myth of Mental Illness*; B., *Oxford Group*; B., *Good Book*.

27. Parker and Dare, *Prayer Can Change*, 179–80.

Since we have embraced the "pernicious doctrine," we have either cultivated childishness or rebellious adolescence (because adolescence is the final attainment of rebellion and one cannot move to true adulthood). Of course, many people have graduated to adulthood, but with no help from the Genesis story. However, we need to complete our understanding of the story of the garden, and self-consciously move against the doubly pernicious effects of not having done so. The need to become mature adults is now more important than ever before.

I am positing that this answer is correct, and this answer is the best I know. The heart of the dilemma of the West is not answered, or answerable apart from it. This unresolved ambiguity in Christian doctrine leaves one in the uncomfortable position of having a certain sympathy with Blake, Shelley, Marx, and Alinsky. They have seen the fall itself as salvation and growth into maturity. However, I would argue that their fall "upward" has instead been a fall into shame and de-glorification.[28]

GLORYING IN OUR SHAME

The doubting Descartes and the Romantic Milton critics have mostly won.[29] They control our major cultural institutions. The primary purpose of almost all of our great universities is to carry through the Cartesian project of doubt and the great Romantic project of rebellion.[30] These institutions

28. The best popular presentation of the Blake/Shelley/Milton theory of the "fall upward" is the movie, *Pleasantville*. It is well-done, clever, entertaining, and includes every element of the Romantic theory, including the all too common idea that the fall had something to do with sex, which it didn't. It goes on to dramatize that being "unfallen" is boring conformism, that marriage is a trap, and that illicit sex and adultery are the pathways to glory. Milton, by the way, got the sex issue quite right. His depiction of love making after the fall is that for the first time it was filled with anxiety and much psychic misery *as a result of the fall*. *Pleasantville* is very worthwhile as an entertaining fantasy illustration of the most devastating and damaging myth of the nineteenth, twentieth, and now early twenty-first centuries. This myth has been a major source of many, if not most, of the miseries of the modern world. "Pleasantville (film)."

29. One of the primary burdens of Michael Polanyi's magisterial volume is to show that it is impossible for knowledge to begin with doubt. In order to doubt something, one must already believe something is true. One must have a platform from which to doubt in the first place. Belief always precedes doubt, and it is not true that science, in living practice, ever makes doubt primary. Doubt is a secondary (albeit necessary) epistemological moment always following something that is believed. Polanyi, *Personal Knowledge*, 269–298.

30. Of course, there are exceptions to this generality. However, one cannot speak if

are controlled by those who have bypassed the Tree of Life; they have first eaten from The Tree of Knowledge. The very ideal of this knowledge is not knowledge that has as its foundation gratitude, joy, and pure receptiveness from God, but rather, knowledge founded on autonomy, doubt and rebellion against authority, and especially, God's authority. The professor is above all a critic.[31] He is one who "sees through" all traditionally received knowledge, especially knowledge founded in revelation. Our universities specialize in stripping us of all of the clothing that God has covered us with.

All cultures in the past have had various kinds of psychic and spiritual clothing. Aristocrats and royalty clearly were clothed with special honor. The peasant, too, was rooted and grounded—he "fit" and belonged.

If we think now about the modern university, a place like Harvard is almost an intellectual nudist colony. Oddly, there is no one more "clothed" than a Harvard professor, clothed with all of the dignity and honor and prestige of that mighty institution. However, unlike a king in the past, his glory is not the glory of being clothed with a numinous splendor that now others can bask in, but his glory is the glory of seeing through all of the numinous to nothing. He is a better, more prestigious, nihilist than all others in the culture. His (or her) peculiar honor is that they have the special and luminous office of being glory, honor, and apparel destroyers. A place like Harvard has become an institution that is especially given to "glorying in our shame."

"OH GAWD"

The use of the above phrase may well date what I write here. It will not date it because the sentiment is likely to go out of fashion anytime soon, but because the cultural phrase used to identify what is felt is likely to change, just as all fashions are ephemeral. The above blasphemy captures quite well exactly what the sophisticate feels when in the presence of those who are insufficiently motivated by critique, doubt, and rebellion against divine

---

one does not employ some generalities, and this is one that is not difficult to see and understand as very generally true.

31. Modernism happened when Adam shook his fist in God's face, and told him he was running the show now. Late modernity happened when Adam realized that for some time, he had been groveling in the dust all day before a serpent, and doing whatever it was that the serpent wanted. Postmodernism began when Adam suddenly realized how ridiculous his situation was, declared it inevitable, and decided he would feel better if only he could become eloquently cynical about it, and affect a stance of detached irony.

authority. "Oh Gawd" and, "They believe that in flyover country."[32] The sophisticate is ashamed at what is seen as naive faith and simple belief. To hear the Bible as authoritative and to gather around that book in the community of the church (that very imperfect institution) is the kiss of death in sophisticated circles. Try an experiment; even just a thought experiment. See what the effect of saying the name of Jesus Christ is in such circles. The name of Jesus, unless used as a blasphemy, is one that makes the face flush with embarrassment. Not too long ago, to be a witness for that name in sophisticated circles earned one the disapprobation of being "a Christer,"[33] something to be avoided like the plague.

NAUSEA

> Jesus said, "Whoever is ashamed of me, and my words...of him the son of man will be ashamed when he comes in his glory." (Mark 8:38)

Alvin Plantinga said this about the great European existentialist, Martin Heidegger:

> This desire for autonomy, self-definition, and self creation can assume quite remarkable proportions: according to Richard Rorty, Martin Heidegger felt guilty about living in a world he hadn't

---

32. Flyover country, flyover states, and Flyoverland are Americanisms describing the parts of the United States between the East and the West Coasts. The terms, which are often used pejoratively, refer to the interior regions of the country passed over during transcontinental flights—e.g. flights between the nation's two major urban agglomerations, the Northeastern Megalopolis and Southern California. "Flyover country" thus refers to the part of the country that many Americans only view by air and never actually see in person on ground level.

33. Compare the sophisticated cultural response to Alger Hiss over against Whittaker Chambers. In spite of overwhelming evidence that Hiss was indeed a spy for the Soviet Union, upon release from prison, he was almost instantly issued invitations from prestigious institutions to teach. Chambers wrote one of the great volumes of the twentieth century, entitled *Witness*. It was always meant to be a double *entendre*. It meant on the one hand that he was a witness against Hiss, but far more deeply, he was a witness for Jesus Christ, in whom he had come to believe after leaving the Communist Party. Chambers became an everlasting embarrassment on our great university campuses and other sophisticated institutions. He stopped basing his life on Romantic rebellion and Cartesian doubt, and began basing it on the knowledge of Jesus Christ as found in his church and word; this was unforgivable.

himself created, refused to feel at home in any such world, and couldn't stand the thought that he was not his own creation.[34]

The great French existentialist, Jean-Paul Sartre, said this about himself in his book *Nausea*:

> I exist because I think...and I can't stop myself from thinking. At this very moment—if I exist, it is because I am horrified at existing. I am the one who pulls myself from the nothingness to which I aspire: the hatred, the disgust of existing.[35]

Dr. John Frame, Professor of Apologetics and Systematic Theology at Reformed Theological Seminary in Orlando, Florida—and my professor and teacher from many years ago—had this to say about the idea of propositional revelation:

> I can see the whole history of liberal theology from 1650 (Spinoza) to the present as a series of rejections of "propositional revelation." They have many different reasons for rejecting an inspired book, but they are unanimous in rejecting it—and in little else. This seems to be a fundamental stumbling block to academic-type unbelief.[36]

And, finally, a quote about Frank Buchman:

> When he [Buchman] first came to Oxford, men wanted to spend hours with him discussing their intellectual doubts...he used to say, "What some people need is not a feather duster but a rotor street broom and some strong disinfectant."[37]

Sartre's quote, and the quote about Heidegger are shocking but revelatory. They understood and felt the consequence of disobeying and departing from God. Both of them found existence unbearable because both of

34. Plantinga, *Warranted Christian Belief*, 261.

35. Sartre, *Nausea*.

36. Dr. John Frame in a personal letter to me.

37. Howard, *Frank Buchman's Secret*, 88. Frank Buchman was the initiator of the Oxford Group, which later became Moral Re-Armament (1938), the parent group of Alcoholics Anonymous. Awakening broke out in Oxford after Buchman arrived there in 1918, and a very notable group of his converts who were Rhoads Scholars, a few years later did a world evangelistic tour with him and were the foundation of the Oxford Group. It became a world encompassing movement. Malcom Muggeridge said that in his opinion, the Oxford Group constituted the only genuine Christian awakening that England experienced in the twentieth century. I was personally touched by the movement in the late 1960s; both my life and Christian faith were quite transformed.

them weighed the true cost of godlessness. Sartre's *Nausea* preceded his great theoretical works and formed the foundation for them. He took Descartes to his end and conclusion. Descartes was a child playing with matches; Sartre lived long enough to burn the forest down. For Sartre, thinking implies existence ("I think, therefore I am.") and this thinking and existence are founded on revolt, and revolt has become revulsion. It is sickening, and he cannot stop it. It goes on and on and on and it is utterly unbearable. Heidegger longed for the full escape to complete and absolute autonomy, but he could not do this. The full possibility of complete self-creation and creation of all that was around and about him was a logical absurdity. He was "thrown" into existence and found himself a squatter, a trespasser, a criminal on someone else's property. His very body was not his own, and he could not stand the fact that his own being did not come from himself.

More recently, Darwinism has been the foil that has been tried to escape the real consequences of Creation[38] ("It is now possible to be an intellectually satisfied atheist . . .") but prior to Darwin, a Kantian outlook in which the human mind does its best to be the creator was the gambit that was tried. In both cases, they are desperate measures. Both Heidegger and Sartre built entire philosophies specializing on the despair, the disgust, the revulsion, of the final impossibility and absurdity of self-creation. Nobody can do everything, and everybody has to specialize on some form of specific labor, some specific task. Their specialty, their sphere of sweat and daily effort was to concentrate all of their powers on what it felt like when an unrepentant Adam was cast out of the garden. Heidegger, in his subtlety in examining all of the feeling states and forms of existence of *"Dasein"*— who is "thrown into being"—is like a great Pascal without God, matching Pascal's finesse and acuteness in examining states of existence, but ending in and glorying in hopelessness. Both Heidegger and Sartre tried to build everything on finding some way out other than bowing the knee, and offering gratitude and thanksgiving to God for life and existence.[39] They unveiled and lived the real consequence of Cartesian doubt.

38. The amount of information that is transmitted in so much as a single cell brought Antony Flew to surrendering his atheism. Darwinism has to contend that something on the order of the *Encyclopedia Britannica* could happen by chance, and that in a relatively short period of time. Flew finally threw in the towel, but most Darwinists are content to maintain this, and continue to maintain the final and absolute meaninglessness and purposelessness of it all in the end as well. Flew and Varghese, *There Is A God*.

39. In a fascinating turn of events, Heidegger makes a good deal of the meaning and necessity of gratitude in this volume. He is too acute an observer to not see this most

Intellectuals (most being far less consistent than Heidegger and Sartre) live by the word. In an Enlightenment and post-Enlightenment world, the intellectual's word is the word of critique, doubt, and rebellion.[40] He must deconstruct the world as God's creation, and then, he must reconstruct all phenomena as the re-creation of his own word. He must regard his word as creative, and his temptation to consider his own word as infallible is very strong. His words are the new Bible in their own little way. At the same time, once anything has been removed in the mind from the created order, for which the only appropriate response is gratitude, that thing becomes a deep object of disgust and nausea. What Sartre so eloquently said about nausea becomes true of the word as well as things. It is the word that vests naked things with "essence," or meaning. This is unbearable, though, and is experienced as so many fig leaves. Here we have the great (and typical) schizophrenic split: the infallible intellectual comes to hate his own word. The intellectual is actually a sniveling weakling in competition with God, and he resents his own weakness and inferiority, but covers it over. He begins to live by a kind of ubiquitous resentment, but then he glories in his resentment or as Nietzsche termed it *ressentiment*.[41] He is nauseated, but he represses his self-hatred, and so must project his own nausea outward. He

---

central reality of human existence, but too committed to atheism to be able to ground it in any adequate way. It is an odd self-contradiction for one committed to self-creation and another addition to the ultimate absurdity of our being. Heidegger, *What Is This?*

40. I was going to use the phrase, "post-Christian world," but have changed it, because I do not believe this. Ironically, Jesus Christ has set the entire agenda of the modern world. One is either for or against him, and when we say "post-Christian," all we really mean is that our culture is arranged all around being "against him," or attempting to ignore him. But this is self-defeating. Already in admitting we are anti-Christ, we have, in a backhanded way, acknowledged his triumph. The glorious stanzas of the Ps 72 tell the deeper truth of his long-range victory: "May he have dominion from sea to sea, and from the River to the ends of the earth!" vs. 8, RSV) There is nowhere left to go after Jesus. The archaic world is blocked off, and the future, if there is to be one, can only be through him. It is well to remember that the very idea of "future" was found originally in the Hebrew Scriptures, and nowhere else. Serious authors who have tried to fathom a future without God, for a long time, have given up on "utopias," and have given us instead, "dystopias," most notably, Huxley's *Brave New World,* Orwell's *1984,* and C. S. Lewis's *That Hideous Strength* (which is actually a retelling of the story of the Tower of Babel and the overthrowing of the nightmares of the previous two dystopias).

41. This concept was later given a remarkable Christian interpretation by Max Scheler in *Ressentiment*. Nietzsche, *Genealogy of Morals*, 33–36.

especially hates the Bible, unless it can be made over in his own image. The Bible, as the inspired Word, is his own primary competitor.[42]

In a Kantian epistemology, what could language possibly signify or symbolize? Kantianism is the great protection from what lay beyond. The noumenal realm (to our great relief) is completely unknowable.[43] Phenomena can only symbolize other phenomena, and what is the point of that, or at most, it is to a very limited point, unless the point is to banish God? Everything is rendered to "nothing but," which is the same as being naked. The intellectual's word is paradoxically, finally, in vain. I am not sure that it is not almost formulaically true that Enlightenment equals nakedness, which is shame. To then make bearable the unbearable, we must glory in our shame and pretend that what is shameful is august and resplendent. Both Heidegger and Sartre try very hard to crow about "freedom," "authenticity," and how we create our own meaning in meaninglessness.

If we glory in our shame, the last thing the "ring leaders" want (who profit the most from this) is a word from beyond. That word would make manifest our shame and destroy our glory in our shame. Since that word is inescapable, we must hide.

Here is a modern and postmodern schizophrenia: the university intellectual is both completely manifest in shamelessness (glorying in his shame) and completely hidden (to hide from the word) all at once. There is nothing the intellectual is more embarrassed by than "God's words," in the form of a completed and authoritative Bible. Dr. Frame's quotation above briefly outlines for us much of the theological labors of the last 450 years. We will do and say most anything (particularly if it can be marked

---

42. This reminds me of "Criswell's Ditty," a little joke attributed to the great Texas Evangelical preacher: "Behold, Jesus met with the five famous and illustrious theologians, Barth, Bonhoeffer, Brunner, Bultmann, and Tillich. And He said unto them, 'And, who do you say that I am?' Barth, Bonhoeffer, Brunner, Bultmann and Tillich all chorused back their learned answer. They replied, 'Thou art the Ground of Being, the Leap of Faith into the Impenetrable Unknown, the Confrontation With the Infinitude of Inherent Experience.' And Jesus looked into the eyes of Barth, Bonhoeffer, Brunner, Bultmann and Tillich and said, 'Flesh and blood has revealed this unto you.'"

43. To quote Dr. Frame, concerning Kant: "So, then, Descartes and Rousseau. And Kant. The more I read Kant, the more I am convinced that the central thing there is for man to be in the place of God. Plato thought that the forms of experience were in a world beyond us. Kant thinks they are imposed by our minds upon experience. Keep in mind that in one sense form is all there is. Matter, the raw stuff (roughly equivalent to the Kantian noumenal) has no qualities and therefore is really nothing. So we are the creators of everything there is. And, of course, for Kant, we are also the authors of the moral law, and the authors of our own salvation."

out as "clever" or "brilliant") to obscure a clear word. But Jesus unveils for us the real motive in the first quote. Fallen man is ashamed of his words and we are fleeing.[44]

Our era (every era is at least slightly different) has concocted a brew that is a mixed potion of shamelessness and pride, intended to medicate our age's de-glorified, de-flowered state; it is a deadly brew. Intellectuals first de-flower us, and then claim that only they can restimulate any sense of worth and value to what has been reduced to little more than complex chemical junk.

Frank Buchman, in the fifth quote, went to the heart of cure. The complex doubts of intellectuals often arise out of simple things and desires that are not so glorious (and not so complex or profound). We have plenty to be ashamed of in his presence, but all attempts to flee are useless. One cannot flee omnipresence.[45]

I have either heard, or read several accounts of atheists recently, in which one of their primary complaints about God's existence is their desire for some privacy. "Who wants an omniscient God watching you all the time . . . ?"[46] The wish seems to be for some non-divine supreme court (perhaps with current day intellectuals on the bench) to find a cosmic "right to privacy" for its occupants. Alas, there is no such court. It is impossible to explain to an outsider, that once one is *in* the household of faith, that the experience of God's presence is not an oppressive experience in the least, but a great and everlasting comfort. God is not only high and lifted up (greater than the whole of his creation combined, so his presence *can* be terrifying) but also is more humble than any mere human being. He is literally and incomparably the most delightful and wonderful of all companions. He is

44. Max Picard is as perceptive and insightful as either Heidegger or Sartre, but he wrote from the perspective of one who has found rest in him. Anxiety and flight are exactly what characterize modern man, and Picard has written an extremely perceptive phenomenology of this. Picard, *Flight From God.*

45. "Whither shall I go from Thy Spirit? Or whither shall I flee from thy presence? If I ascent to heaven, thou art there! If I make my bed in Sheol, thou art there!" (Ps 139:7–8)

46. Bethell, *Eric Hoffer,* 204–05. I also heard this sentiment expressed by Christopher Hitchens in a debate with Dinesh DeSousa at the University of Colorado a few years ago. Do we really welcome the idea of an omniscient deity minutely scrutinizing our lives? As a possibility, Hoffer considered it to be more discomforting than hopeful, "The most awful thing that could happen would be to discover that God really exists," he wrote. An omniscient God would know our secrets. Therefore, "to those who believe in God and a hereafter there is no escape from the scheme of things. They are eternally trapped." Suicide offered no escape.

the source of all glory and wonder, which he longs to share with his now denuded creatures and creation. This is *why* Christ came.

Yes, Saul Alinsky can be saved. He need only crawl through the eye of a needle, which is of course, impossible. But that is what Christ did for us. Even rich men, and even intellectuals, and political radicals can be saved (Luke 18:24–27). He bids you come in, and find the refreshment of his presence, and the wonder of his word. He speaks even to you.

If you do not come in, even in the day of opportunity (now), you have not experienced the end of God's voice. One day, you will hear the voice of terror. "Depart from me. I never knew you" (Matt 7:23). Or you *can* hear, "Fear not, you will not be ashamed; you will be not confounded . . . but with everlasting love I will have compassion on you, says the Lord your Redeemer" (Isa 54:4, 8). Accept the offer and close the deal. The time is now; it is upon you.

5

God Speaks, Therefore I Am

A NUMBER OF YEARS ago, a young Alvin Plantinga established his very considerable reputation as a philosopher with the publication of *God and Other Minds*. It was as a philosophical work, brilliant in every way. It had what has since come to be expected of Plantinga: his hallmark of very closely reasoned argumentation. However, what really made the book successful was its cleverness—one might even say its cheekiness. Plantinga wrote a book examining all of the objections to Thomas' arguments for God's existence, and granted many of them as possibly valid. But then he turned around and demonstrated that the very arguments against God's existence work in almost an across the board way against the existence of any other minds or persons. If you maintain the refutation of the arguments in a rigorous way, you are left completely by yourself in the universe. It made the world a very lonely place for aggressive atheists. Plantinga achieved a very great *tour de force*.

Plantinga did not really rehabilitate the proofs. He is not convinced that one can prove God's existence in this way. Rather, his point is that you cannot prove the existence of other minds in this way, or any other way, either. Nobody really believes that thinking that other people exist is irrational, and common sense would tell us that a man who was a consistent and sincere solipsist would be a madman. Plantinga has gone on to make a career of this point. He maintains that there are many things that one is entirely justified in believing without a shred of rigorous logical proof. He says that I am entitled to believe in my own existence, the existence of my neighbor, the existence of the external world, the existence of the past, and many other things, as well as the existence of God. There is something to this.

There is a word that one must be very careful about, and see if it is being used in an honest way, or to cover up a crime. That word is "obviously." If I am making an argument, and I suddenly come upon a part of my argument that is very weak, then I am very liable to insert the word, "obviously" in that place, hoping no one will notice, and that they will be swept along by my previous momentum. "Obviously" is what you say when you can't think of how to make a good argument; ultimately, this is quite dishonest.

However, there are other times when "obviously" is used very honestly. There are some things so plain that it would be impossible to think of an argument for them, or even give a very clear articulation of what it is that you mean. Life really is made up of these kind of uses of the word "obviously." The worst thing is if someone shows up who says you can't think or do a thing unless you first can define it and then come up with some good argument for it. Organizations sometimes get seadog lawyers in them who think this is the way to operate, and they make life very difficult.[1] Who would tell a family that they could not have an after-dinner "family counsel" to make some important family decisions unless they could first write a constitution that could justify such a proceeding? Or who would be such a fool as to tell a young couple that they couldn't fall in love unless they could first define it? It may be very useful for there to be people in the world who do philosophize about such things. Political philosophers and wise people about love and marriage are useful, too, but the things they philosophize about do not depend upon the philosophers to make them happen or be real in the first place.

To carry the point on a bit, imagine what life would be like if the body and nervous system did not do most things automatically for you, or if you did not have any habits. If you had to think about making your heart beat the way you have to think about doing your income tax, you would certainly die before the first day was out. If you had to think about all the things that you do habitually, like driving a car, or riding a bicycle, then you would never have any time or energy left to do any of the things you really want to do. In fact, life would probably be impossible. It is a very good thing, then, that you do not have to think about many things you do; they just happen. Nevertheless, somebody or something has to think about them. They really do not happen all by themselves. That is why you have a nervous system and a brain. The rest of your body is very grateful that somebody is in charge.

This is exactly how the great body of our knowledge and beliefs actually function. They are automatic and work all by themselves, and you are not even aware of them. A man who goes around constantly thinking about

1. The great seadog lawyer of our time was W. K. Clifford in his 1876 essay, "The Ethics of Belief," in which he argues, "It is wrong always, everywhere, and for anyone, to believe anything upon insufficient evidence."

them and trying to define and justify them is in the exact same place as the man who goes about always monitoring his pulse or his blood pressure. He is a philosophic hypochondriac. On the other hand, no one really thinks that it is optional whether or not you breathe, or have a pulse. These are very necessary things, as a few minutes absence will demonstrate, and we have doctors for those times that we term emergencies, and we are grateful that they are there. It may well be that there are a body of beliefs that are likewise necessary and not at all optional, and there ought to be someway of determining what those are. Or someone ought to be in charge of letting us know. We may need doctors of wisdom as well.

How does one go about "justifying," that is, establishing an adequate rationale, for such a plethora and network of hidden and underground beliefs and propositions that actually undergird my whole existence? To change the metaphor a bit: is it necessary to understand how and why my computer, my radio, or television, actually work before I turn them on and use them and enjoy them? Should I doubt the real existence of the Bach concerto I am currently enjoying from the local FM station if the workings, or even existence, of radio waves are a perfect mystery to me? Plantinga says, "No. You are quite justified at this moment in your current state of ignorance. Go ahead and enjoy the music."

However, this notion of "no need for justification" can be so weak and pallid that there is no real compass or direction. I may not need to understand all the workings of the computer to first use it. I do need some insight to know that it is not a doorstop, or a car jack, and I do need to know how to turn it on. Steve Jobs, who had many more conscious insights into computers than I do, might have some helpful insights for a novice like myself. The great problem is that you are not sure if there is a Steve Jobs (or a cosmic Steve Jobs), or if *anyone* in the end is in charge. One can be left without any real compass to give any guidance at all. All kinds of beliefs may very well be "rational" and in some sense justified, but there is no single belief that is very compelling, either. In the history of philosophy, if Hegel is something like the great socialist of the philosophical world who is sure that he can centrally plan everything, then this perspective becomes the great libertarian outlook. The philosophic libertarian is quite sure that everything will run itself with no one in charge at all. All kinds of ideas and beliefs may be perfectly respectable, but none of them are very obligatory. This would be a philosophy that is a gentleman's philosophy and makes no real demands on anybody.[2]

2. Carson, *Gagging of God*, 186–88.

For fun, let's try an experiment. Let's give the world to the prigs for a moment. Let's give the world to the people who demand a definition and an argument for most everything. Then where are we? In all likelihood, the prigs are in some level of trouble. It is one thing to go around demanding such rigor of everyone else, but surely the prig is going to have to have his turn at it too, and then he will have as hard a time as everyone else. Someone could ask him for a proof that everyone needs to have proofs, and then for a good solid definition of proofs to boot. The philosophic prig is a busybody, always sticking his nose in where it is not welcome, and furthermore, he is not needed and does not succeed. Hegel is more like the prig, and he fails. But does the libertarian do much better?

What has been demonstrated is the need for authority. For philosophic libertarianism, God seems to serve no real epistemological purpose at all. If God is God, then there can be no doubt that he is, or ought to be, the one in charge of all the automatic things and ideas that lurk under the surface for everyone everywhere. Justification, then, becomes his domain. It is perfectly right that people shouldn't have to go about always being bothered about that. But somebody needs to be, and God seems the proper candidate. For the philosophic libertarians, it seems that about all God has to do is to be believed to exist, and to democratically be given some rights along with all kinds of other beliefs that people might have. In this universe, God just seems to hang around. He is basically unemployed, or at least drastically underemployed. He has not been given a job consonant with his abilities.

Authority is the weakest link in the libertarian chain (as it is for all kinds and brands of libertarian). If I am justified in believing that God exists, then surely I am also justified in the knowledge that God has absolute authority to determine what my beliefs and everyone else's beliefs in the world ought to be. If God exists, then a necessary corollary to his existence is his absolute authority. If all of this is wrong, then it is wrong to state that I am justified in believing in God's existence, because his existence would entail this. Or, the libertarian just believes in a different God who is only a god. How can you believe in a God (god) who doesn't press obligation on people, indeed on everybody? People sometimes talk about "my God" this, or "my God" that, as if he were kept up on the fireplace mantle in a bottle.

One can be quite modest about philosophy's (and reason's) capacities, and this is perhaps good. This sort of philosophy is, on the other hand, perhaps too proud to let God take his rightful place. As is often the case, one kind of modesty may be cover for another kind of boastfulness. In a backhanded sort of way, this kind of philosophy in effect tells God to mind his own business. The universe and everybody in it can get on quite well, really, without him, thank you.

The difficulty here is that justification is an affair strictly of the independent human mind. It is all a matter of self-talk. I talk to myself and reassure myself that I am there, my neighbor is there, the world is there, and the past is no fiction. But self-talk is inadequate. Justification begins and ends there. The result is pretty much a two by four universe that is not very interesting, and doesn't go very far. And this world of philosophy, a world of "obviously," is, in the end, not using "obviously" in an honest way. For if warrant and justification are measured out as purely affairs of the human mind, then in the end there is no compelling reason to believe that I exist, or you exist, or that two plus two is four is not an illusion, along with all of reason. The best one can do at that point is to simply point out that circularly these are things that everybody "obviously" knows. If these things are true, it is because God has made them so, and for no other reason. One cannot escape the necessity to not just begin with self-talk, and not to just exercise the human mind, but to begin by submitting my word to the Bible as God's word as the basis for justification of all knowledge. If justification and warrant for belief are autonomous activities, then in the end they are also futile activities.

In the end, philosophic libertarianism reminds me of Erasmus. He was learned, witty, pleasant, and a gentleman. Martin Luther was a very different kind of man, and he was no gentleman. If Luther was to be healed of his very considerable trouble of soul, it was going to take much stouter medicine than the sort that Erasmus had. Indeed, Erasmus was probably even incapable of understanding Luther's real complaints. An interesting experiment in our day would be to think of someone analogously epistemologically troubled—maybe a Foucault.

Luther had to cross a Rubicon—the strong doctrine that man's efforts are worthless in the end—and Erasmus was not interested in following. Justification can only happen when it is wholly a Divine act to which man adds nothing. All he can do is receive it. I think, in the end, warrant and justification for anything we know is at least similar. Purely human lifting is wholly inadequate. There is no strong man who can lift the world, or break the seals, except for one (Rev 5:1–5). According to one modern *savant*, even Atlas shrugged. There is no mere man (or god) to be trusted. There are helpful distinctions, and helpful qualifications that can be made. A very powerful *negative* case concerning *what has not been proven or demonstrated* has been put on the table. But justification, *real* justification for knowledge, is more than a mere man with his own self-talk and naked intellect can give. In the end, warrant for anything we know is at least analogous to Luther's experience. Human cleverness by itself is inadequate. The libertarians are clever and elegant if they are anything. They have persuasively shown how laughably inadequate the objectors to Christian revelation and thought have been. We can only enjoy them and applaud them for their laudable efforts. To positively provide justification, though, real justification for knowledge is more than a mere man with his own self-talk can give. It has to be founded upon the Divine act, and upon Divine speech. God *has spoken*, and we must submit to, receive, and build upon that wonder and that authority. This is only given to us finally and with adequate completeness in Holy Scripture and nowhere else. This is the Rubicon that must be crossed, and Scripture leads us to the ark that must be boarded.[3]

CROSSING THE RUBICON

If God exists, does his existence entail the prescriptive obligation to believe in him, and believe him? If so, how is that obligation communicated to us? Does God conduct a lifelong dialogue or dispute with his subjects to bring them into compliance with that obligation?

Nobody has rights that can be exercised apart from a very strong state that will guarantee them and make them possible in the first place; furthermore, one must become a citizen in order to exercise those rights. To be a citizen, one must take an oath of loyalty. There is one nation in which everyone is commanded, and has an obligation to come in and sign up (1 Pet 2:9).

---

3. Plantinga was aware that something stronger was necessary beyond what was left as a vacuum when he attacked justification for knowledge that had previously been built on what is now termed "foundationalism" in *God and Other Minds*. He developed the notion of "warrant and proper function" in a series of books with those words in their titles, as a replacement for the previous idea of justification. Again, it is immensely clever, and extremely helpful, but it is only a base hit when what is needed is a home run. It is another form of natural theology and still does not take with adequate seriousness the authority of God's speech to us in Holy Scripture. And while he does demonstrate to us (for example) that Darwinism hardly makes for an adequate grounding for true knowledge, he never gets further than asserting that "proper function flourishes in the soil of theism." Again, it has all of the cleverness of Erasmus, with none of the stoutness of Luther. The Rubicon is still there.

So how does one cross the Rubicon? One gets on the Ark. And what is the Ark? Everyone knows the story: God told Noah to build the Ark in order to escape his coming judgment. He gathered his family, and all of the animals and he did so. In Pet 3:21, the Apostle Peter tells us enough that we know that the ark is a type, a symbol, of the church.[4] One now "boards" the church, which is that community gathered around the Bible, in order to escape the coming judgment of God. The Bible is God's speech to his people to give them enough knowledge to now "build an ark" and to navigate through the seas of this world, to arrive at the country of the king on the other shore safely. What was Noah's foundation for knowledge, true knowledge? It was what was his Bible, which we have portions preserved for us in Gen 6–9. We have a completed Bible. What is termed the New Testament is the final installment, in this world, of that inspired communication to the human race. It is through this word that we have a "normative" text—speech that is from God—that tells us what we need to know as an adequate foundation for all of human knowledge. The ark is the church, the flood is baptism, and the Bible is our guide. Let's examine this.

GOD, WOMEN, AND GENIUSES

How convenient it must be to be God. God has the ability to know everything all at once, in one fell swoop. That must be nice, but it is a capability that we lack (and anyway, it entails a lot of additional responsibility that I would be loath to have). The closest that human beings come to this attribute of God's is to be found in both women and geniuses. In the days of sexism, when men indulged in caviling against women, they often accused them of "not thinking"—that is, not thinking in a linear fashion. The steps were all skipped over and the conclusion was simply come to in some incomprehensible way. What is especially humbling to men, especially men very proud of thinking things through step-by-step, is when they are shown up to be wrong, and "woman's intuition" simply reaches the proper conclusion effortlessly, with no thought of justifying the outcome step-by-step.[5]

4. I am assuming, here, that the ark was also a real historical fact. When one is a Christian, one is not forced to choose between the literal or the symbolic. All literal facts are also filled with symbol. God created by speaking (Gen 1:1–3). This implies that grammar is the very structure of the universe, and hence the reality in, around, and through every fact in the universe. This is the foundation of the possibility of virtually all of the arts, which depend fundamentally upon the symbolic.

5. Men and women may have both of these ways of thinking inside of them, to varying

When the man's careful progression reaches the wrong conclusion very carefully, it is humbling indeed. How many men have wished they had been less proud. A "woman's intuition" is actually quite liberated, and is closer to God's ways than is the man's clunky and methodical way. God does not "think." He knows everything in one vast intuition. God is however, rarely railed against, because he is too much "like a woman." God generally suffers from the malady of being thought "too male."

The other category of humans that especially resemble God in this way are geniuses. Proverbially, genius simply intuits an outcome, a theory, a book, a symphony, "all at once." All at once, it comes into existence and is full grown. Mozart apparently could hear a whole symphony in his head "all at once." After he heard it, he seemed simply to transcribe it, and there it was, perfect, with just the right number of notes, none too few, none too many. It was as close to perfection as fallen humanity is permitted.

It is also the case that God has revealed himself in a very careless way, running rough shod over men's careful steps that he ought to have employed. Just how can we come to "know God?" ask the philosophers. What careful steps ought to be gone through: steps one, two, three, all in precise and comfortable order? Unfortunately, God seems to have skipped over Logic 101 and such careful methodology has been has been run over rough shod. This nice, careful, methodology has come to be termed "foundationalism" in recent years. Some years earlier, Cornelius Van Til called it "blockhouse methodology."[6] It means I start carefully with a very certain starting point, and slowly build a great tower upward and upward, until I finally reach God at the very top.[7] Some would now say, as Van Til was saying many years ago, that this tower was only a Tower of Babel, and it never could yield an intelligible outcome. Was that starting point *really* so

---

degrees. How much these differences are inborn, and how much they are culturally and environmentally determined remains an interesting question. Hard evidence is lacking.

6. Dr. Cornelius Van Til of Westminster Theological Seminary

7. The picture that comes to my mind is the philosopher as "The Cat in the Hat," from the great Dr. Seuss classic, doing his balancing act while standing on a ball and the next thing you know, he has come down with a BUMP! And so it is with the philosophers with their balancing act, attempting to also dance on what is little better than a ball. They also come down with a BUMP! The true picture, however, is that the cat with his hat, and everything he was trying to balance, and the ball he was standing on, and then finally the very gravitational force that brought him down, were themselves all revelations of the God he was trying to prove in the first place, and he ought to have known that! Seuss, *Cat in The Hat*, 18–20.

certain and clear in and of itself, and by itself, so that a tower could safely be constructed upon it?[8]

God after all, is *supposedly* uncertain, vague and unknown. So I must begin with something that is certain, real, concrete, and not vague. Let us begin with reason, or another starting point might be the stuff immediately in front of me, like this table and these chairs. These are commonly termed, "facts." If I begin there, and then reason upward and outward from those "certain" starting points, and look far enough, I will reach the conclusion of God, if I am clear-headed and clever enough.

Is any one starting point really "foundational," and really necessary? Where is one really to start? Is reason really reasonable? Are facts really facts? What strange questions. The indubitable is difficult to find and this takes us back to our opening chapters. One must begin somewhere, one must assume something, or one is just fit for the madhouse. If reason is not reasonable, and facts are not facts, how can one even begin to comprehend or to think? Universally, unless one just begins and ends with madness, some things must be assumed and cannot be proven; some things are "obvious."[9]

What if (and again, "what ifs?" are very helpful for us to "try on something for size" to see how it works) God was not particularly interested in all of our attempts to get to him as some sort of conclusion, and he, rather, revealed himself to us in some way that undergirded everything else, all at once? What if the "conclusion" he was interested in was as himself as the "end" in the sense of purpose behind everything that he already undergirded, and what if he revealed himself in that undergirding? God, after all, may not be such a bore as to have nothing more to do than just hang around and "exist." It is a rare thing for anyone of anyone's acquaintance to see their own person's primary meaning as being that of existing. Persons are generally occupied and are interested in what does occupy them. Perhaps God is the same. There might after all be some point or purpose to what he has done in creating everything.

Let me start with another kind of circle.

Everything in our lives is always in a certain kind of circle. Oddly, it seems we can't begin unless we have already begun. This is so, because we are neither eternal nor infinite. If one is eternal and infinite, then by definition, one never begins. If one is in a stream of time and finite, then unless one is the very dot of the very beginning, then one is already in the flowing

8. This question is taken up in chapter 8.

9. The question is then, "How do I ground the obvious?"

stream at the moment of consciousness, in spite of one's own beginning. Every beginning reflected on assumes that we are already going. All we can really do is begin to notice more and more that perhaps once upon a time we were at a stop, or at a perfect beginning, but now in our consciousness, we are already going sixty miles an hour. Or, to change the metaphor a bit, we never did "take off" in the plane. We were already in the air, 25,000 feet up and on our way to a destination at six hundred miles per hour, and we simply began to notice at some point. If we insist on always "beginning at the beginning," then we are never in the air, but have to go back to the ground, and then construct the plane and the airport, but we cannot even stop there. We must account for and create the factory that built the plane, produce the concrete that made the airport, and then go back behind that to the iron ore and bauxite that made the steel and aluminum that made the plane, and the elements that made the concrete. You get the picture.

Instead of starting with a bare and naked, and undetermined starting point, we begin with an already existing and moving product. We actually can only (in some sense) *begin* with God. And low and behold, it is not just God, but God as a speaking God. This is at the outset. It was already given. It was given in a vast swoop, and is known already in some coherent completeness.

"In the beginning was the Word, and the Word was with God, and the Word was God" (John 1:1). This is the "prologue" to the Gospel of John. It is the very first sentence given in that gospel.

Now, if I am suggesting that that is a *beginning* point, I can hear the complaints already. "You can't just start there. To believe that is a conclusion, not a starting point. Why should I believe *that* any more than I might believe the Qur'an, or The Book of Mormon?[10] I have to have reasons given to me to believe any of that." Yes, but things are not so simple, not so "male," if you will. This is not a beginning point; this is a jumping in point. The way we really know most everything (if not everything) is not step by step, but

10. To give the briefest of answers: neither of those holy books or texts give any grounding or basis for knowledge or life. Allah is a simple monad, a unitarian being and for that reason cannot even know himself, or the world as his creation. He is a blank as much as Aristotle's unmoved mover is. And the Mormon God is only one of many gods. He is arguably not God at all, but a mere god, of which any living man can also become one. Mormonism, therefore, has no God who can provide a single unified decree that gives a single coherent foundation for knowledge. What is ultimate and behind everything is a pluralistic chaos. Islam fails to provide any grounds for diversity, and Mormonism fails to provide any adequate grounding for an ultimate unity. They fail at opposite ends, and cannot so much as account for themselves, or any of the claims that their holy books make for them.

in an "intuition" in which beginning points and conclusions are all wrapped up in each other, and we become conscious of what we are seeking at some point, and insofar as we begin in the midst of life to understand the already moving stream that we are in. Now, in the midst of that stream, step-by-step thinking becomes very helpful and illuminating to enable us to make clear the truth we have apprehended and correct what may be mistakes, or to understand more completely what we have already intuited. Step-by-step thinking does not create the truth in the first place. It is not creative.

Nobody begins life by creating the matter that was the source of the iron and aluminum and concrete that made up the airplane and the airport. No, we find ourselves already in the air, flying at hundreds of miles per hour, with most everything already being given in a full-blown way. Life is lived as an intuition (if not "all at once," then "much at once") and then known and reflected on also in some "all at once," or "much at once," intuition. However, to get a handle on this, we can break things down in more comprehensible bite size pieces that are step-by-step. And *that* can be a *kind* of beginning. So let's begin with this fullness already being given, and leap into the stream that is already flowing.

"IN THE BEGINNING WAS THE WORD, AND THE WORD WAS WITH GOD, AND THE WORD WAS GOD" (JOHN 1:1)

That is a mouthful; a big mouthful. It is, in fact enough bread to fill the universe, or, to change the metaphor somewhat, it encapsulates the universe. Let's start with an "exegesis,"[11] and then an interpretation.[12]

The original Greek means that if we go all the way back to the beginning (Gen 1:1 says, in concert, "In the beginning...") Jesus was already there. It does not mean that there is a beginning to Jesus, but that in the

---

11. "No one has seen God at any time. The only begotten Son, who is in the bosom of the Father, he has declared him" (John 1:18). What is translated as "declared" is the Greek word "exegeted." It means to "unfold, reveal, manifest, make clear." Hence, the Son "exegetes" God (unfolds, reveals, manifests, makes clear). At the Last Supper, we are told "the disciple whom Jesus loved," (presumably John himself) "leaned on Jesus' bosom" (John 13:23). The implication is clear. Just as Jesus, who is in the bosom of God, "exegetes" God, so John "exegetes" Jesus. He is, in other words, competent to write this gospel as a revelation of Jesus Christ.

12. The church has reflected on this passage for centuries. I will be bringing forth especially some of the thoughts that are traceable back to St. Augustine in his trinitarian reflections.

temporal beginning of the world itself, he was already there and existent. He was there *before* the beginning, and we are told, in fact, that he had something to do with that beginning. Beyond that, he was "with" God. Implied in being "with" God, is that he, too, "was God," that he is the same "stuff" or essence as God.

To go back a bit, though, the preposition translated "with" is the Greek preposition, *pros*. The word *pros* is related to another Greek word, *prosopon*. It is the same root: *prosopon* means "face." The implication being given is that God and the Word are facing each other. They are face-to-face. That is the kind of "with-ness" that we are talking about.[13]

In the midst of this context (and the context is eternal and outside of, or before time, and not in time), the Word was spoken. He was spoken by God himself. What God spoke was all that was within him. The Word is the speech of all that was God. The Word is the perfect, and exhaustive autobiography of God. It is not a partial unveiling of himself, but a complete one. No human autobiography could ever approach this. All speech of ourselves is very limited. An almost infinite number of facts and realities would be excluded. Not so with God, though. All is revealed, and everything is spoken.

It is here that things become especially interesting. When we speak, what comes forth is "speech." We speak words into the air, and if another human is present, hopefully, what is spoken "computes," and meaning is conveyed. In the Godhead, while that sort of thing is also a reality, this *initial* speech is more mysterious and more wonderful. This fullness of speech on the part of God issues not just in sentences and paragraphs and a text, but in another person. This is, in the fullest sense, a *living* Word. It issues in the Son, the second person of the Trinity. The implication is that since this is the "Son," he has come forth from the one who is "the Father" (one cannot have a father without a son, or a son without a father). The Son is the *complete* and *total* revelation of the Father. Whatever is in the Father is likewise now in the Son. This is the basis of Jesus telling the disciple Phillip much later in the Gospel of John, "If you have seen me, you have seen the Father" (John 14:9).

Secondly, it is also the case that the Son speaks himself back to the Father. The "reflection" or "outshining" spoken of in Hebrews (where the image is changed somewhat) is reflected, or spoken back to the Father (Heb 1:3). He reflects back to the Father everything that, likewise, is in him. Hence, we see the basis of another assertion that is in the Bible: "God is Love" (1 John 4:8). This is an infinite and eternal dialogue between the

13. Hoeksema, *Reformed Dogmatics*, 146.

Father and the Son, and it is the basis or foundation of the love life that exists within the Godhead himself.

Finally, there is one more mysterious, even baffling and amazing reality that is implied herein. When the Father speaks the Son, and the Son speaks back his being to the Father, it is spoken by the same means whereby we speak. When we speak, we speak by driving breath, or wind, through our larynx. So it is with God. God speaks by the breath of his being. His breath, just like his Word, is another whole person. It is the person of the Holy Spirit. And beyond that, that breath, the person of the Holy Spirit, is (as St. Augustine asserted) the bond that exists between the Father and the Son, or the speaker and the spoken (the Word). The Holy Spirit *is the relationship* between the Father and the Son, and the Spirit is *spirated*, or breathed, between them.[14]

We are accustomed to thinking of a relationship as a nominal thing, an abstraction, an ethereal description of something that does not have a quite real existence in and of itself. It is not a "thing." In God, though, the relationship of God in himself is a person, the Holy Spirit.

All of this is the foundation of all of existence and it constitutes the "ground of all being." This personal reality is the foundation of Van Til's *A Christian Theory of Knowledge*.[15]

GRAMMAR AND THE WORLD

"In the beginning was the Word . . ." God is a speaking God, and language is raised to an ontological level unparalleled anywhere. To follow up, the Bible does really begin at the beginning. Gen 1:1 famously says, "In the beginning, God created the heavens and the earth." Then through the first two chapters, we are told (step-by-step—the men should like that!) how God spoke the world into existence.

This is related to what we see in the Godhead, but now a step down. God is not only speaking himself into existence, from eternity to eternity, but he also speaks in time (and "time" itself is also a creation of his) and he

---

14. The Apostle Paul tells us, "For the Spirit searches everything, even the depths of God" (1 Cor 2:10). Augustine makes a good deal of this passage in developing his doctrine of the Trinity. The Spirit reveals God to God. God knows himself exhaustively. To use Van Til's arresting phrase, "There are no hidden unconscious depths in God." God is exhaustively self-conscious. Van Til, *Psychology of Religion*, 4:161.

15. Van Til, *Christian Theory*.

speaks "stuff" ordered stuff, into existence. He is speaking the world, and the stars, the sun and moon all into existence. This "stuff" is not divine, but will reflect what is divine, and carry within it a "grammar" of God and his complexity, beauty, and glory. What he is creating is a kind of theatre. It is a theatre and a stage for his final creation, which again is not divine, but a reflection of divinity. This reflection is going to be the highest reflection of all, while still remaining not divinity. He is going to create man and woman. These are also "spoken" into existence. This man and woman are termed "the image of God." Nothing is higher on this plain. Perhaps the most distinctive thing about this man and woman, these images of God, is that they are self-conscious, with self-conscious identities, and they are capable of speech. The created order below them is also said to "speak" but it is not a self-conscious speech. It is speech that is *outshined* in a way that precedes consciousness, but can be apprehended by the image of God and self-consciously spoken of to one another and back to God himself.

Immediately, God begins to have a friendship with man. He speaks to man. The old hymn says, "He walks with me, he talks with me, he tells me I am his own."[16] That began right away; God and man enter a dialogue.

So how do we now know God? The Bible says, in two ways. God's *Word* as his spoken revelation (the Bible), or God's *grammar* that is the "essence," or heart of everything that is. It immediately "testifies" to its origin, to its source. Everywhere, everything "speaks" of the God who created it. Everyone is familiar with this. It is the source of people looking on some particularly beautiful mountain setting, or a sunset, or a craggy coast by the seashore, and declaring, "How could anyone not know that God exists when they see this?" It is the reason that an appallingly high percentage of people refuse to be straightforward Darwinists. In Whittaker Chambers' great book, *Witness*, he declares that with the birth of his first child, and seeing the perfect formation of his baby's ear, he came to believe in God from a position of years and years of atheism:

> My daughter was in her high chair. I was watching her eat. She
> was the most miraculous thing that had ever happened in my life.
> I liked to watch her even when she smeared porridge on her face
> or dropped it meditatively on the floor. My eye came to rest on
> the delicate convolutions of her ear—those intricate perfect ears.
> The thought passed through my mind, "No, those ears were not
> created by any chance coming together of atoms in nature (the

16. "In the Garden" by Charles Austin Miles (1913)

Communist view). They could have been created only by immense design." The thought was involuntary and unwanted. I crowded it out of my mind. But I never wholly forgot it or the occasion. I had to crowd it out of my mind. If I had completed it, I should have had to say: Design presupposes God. I did not then know that, at that moment, the finger of God was first laid on my forehead.[17]

The sheer complexity, beauty, and perfection of much that is around us, culminating in man himself, makes believing that all of this evolved by pure chance, impossible, for a very large percentage of people. It does not even require argument; it is known instantly.

It is also true, though, that another percentage of people (far lower than the academy believe should be so), say they do *not* see the hand of God in all of this. They see accidents and chance and nothingness behind everything.

The Bible said this would be so, but gives its own interpretation of this (back to chapter three on ethics). The Apostle Paul said it was because the truth, even though it is seen and known, is "suppressed," or held under.[18] The source of this "not seeing" is not because it cannot be seen and is not seen. The reason is ethical. Man does not want to see, and he has declared both himself and what is the created order to be self-sufficient in some sense, and not needing God. "God is dead" to quote a more recent thinker. We will him to be dead. It is an attempted murder because we believe if he is out of the way, we can have it to ourselves and on our own terms (Matt 21:33–39). But the price of this is that we have put out our own eyes, and now have to live in a world with no truth, or Truth. Without Truth, truth becomes less than a rare entity, and one is left in confusion, meaningless-ness, and finally death. One is finally left in silence. One is left in a position and place of appalling silence. There is no word if there is no Word.

Secondly, precisely because of this inherent refusal and rebellion, the way was prepared through the establishment of the people of Abraham, to be an advent for the coming personally to this world of The Word. This great adventure is narrated for us. The great preparation is usually termed "the Old Testament," followed by the narration of the New Testament, which is the very story of that visit and its aftermath in the founding of his church.

---

17. Chambers, *Witness,* 15–16.

18. "For the wrath of God is revealed from heaven against all ungodliness and un-righteousness of men who suppress the truth in unrighteousness, because what may be known of God is manifest to them. For since the creation of the world his invisible at-tributes are clearly seen, being understood by the things that are made, even his eternal power and Godhead, so that they are without excuse" (Rom 1:18–20).

What is especially interesting here for our purposes is that this visit cul-minated in the final proof of the "suppression" that was spoken to above. Just as the testimony of God and his nature are denied, held under, suppressed, subverted and denied, and finally perverted into something that it is not, so the personal visit on the part of the Word issued in the same treatment. He was killed, and declared guilty by three earthly courts.[19] The irony of ironies is that that death is what undid the very perversion in man that led to such an appalling outcome in the first place. It led to redemption. God proved his case, and then used the outcome to renew a righteous and holy race.

Our methodology is strange, then. Instead of beginning with some-thing "obvious" like facts or reason, we are beginning with what seems ought to be our conclusion. We are beginning with God and his Word, or with God and the Bible. Can one really do this? A better question would be, can we do anything else? Instead of beginning with "facts and reason," we begin with what makes facts and reason possible in the first place. It turns out that facts and reason are not self-evident, self-explanatory, and do not stand on their own. Somebody stands behind them and makes them possible in the first place. That means that gratitude is far the most sensible epistemological stance.

There is now a certain amount of thinking that the birth of modern atheism is rather directly tied to Christian rationalistic apologetics that wanted to begin with some starting point that was "foundational" and cer-tain.[20] If the deep and hidden assumption is that science can test revelation, or that reason based on other foundations, can in an *ultimate* sense, judge God, then what one has granted already is an anti-Christian premise. Rea-son and, following that, science already has overthrown Christian revela-tion with this arrangement. If they can *ultimately* (not proximately, which is a lower matter) *test* revelation, then they do not need the very God they are testing. They already function very nicely without him. He is irrelevant and unnecessary. If the Christian revelation is true, then it is revelation that will at the very lowest assume the functioning of reason. Reason and science could only ask circular questions. Does this revelation itself account for the "reasonableness" of reason, and account for the "workability" of science?

---

19. Those three courts were, the Sanhedrin, Herod, and Pilate. The Sanhedrin repre-sented the Jewish Temple; Herod ironically sat on the Throne of David, which actually rightfully belonged to Jesus who was the linear descendent of David, and Herod was an Edomite usurper; and Pilot represented the fullness of the Roman Empire and Roman justice. All found Jesus guilty. All earthly justice was unrighteous.

20. Buckley, *Origins*.

Lesslie Newbigin suggests that beginning in the twenty-first century, one of the primary tasks of the church will be to be the *defender* of reason and the scientific endeavor against irrationalism.[21] It now turns out that the hidden assumptions of the Enlightenment, and of much previous rationalistic apologetics, could never have come into existence were it not for the previous confidence already given by Christian revelation to reason, and the application of reason to empirical reality. In other words, we now have the oddity that things are actually backwards. The Enlightenment, which thought itself competent to "judge God," cannot itself survive apart from him. To put it another way, humanism has run aground. Reason depends on God and his revelation. If it were the other way around, God and the Bible would indeed have sunk, but beyond that Enlightenment left to its own devises is building on quicksand. If reason has evolved from the primordial chaos, there is no reason to believe in reason. And, one's confidence in reason being applied fruitfully to empirical reality is also undermined. Chaos begets chaos, and order is arbitrary and short lived. Only the Bible as God's word, and the God of the Bible, gives us a basis to "judge all things." Oddly, and in screaming paradox, Enlightenment cannot survive apart from the faith, which it began by rejecting. St. Paul tells us, "The spiritual man judges all things, but is himself to be judged by no one" (1 Cor 2:15).[22]

21. Newbigin, *Truth and Authority*, 54.

22. Of course in the context of Paul's letter to the Corinthians, "the spiritual man" is to be judged by the Scriptures, and by the church, and ultimately by God. This is not carte blanche for epistemological anarchy. Quite the contrary, it is the bulwark against it. The spiritual man is wholly answerable. The autonomous man, by definition, is not.

6

A Couple of Paradoxes

FOR WANT OF A NAIL

> For want of a nail the shoe was lost.
>
> For want of a shoe the horse was lost.
>
> For want of a horse the rider was lost.
>
> For want of a rider the battle was lost.
>
> For want of a battle the kingdom was lost.
>
> And all for the want of a horseshoe nail.

THE ABOVE RHYME IS not only a fun little poem, but it is also very good philosophy. It points to human limitation that is all too distressing.

The character of life is that one never has everything under control. And no matter how many responsible decisions one makes, there are always a series of "unintended consequences" that follow in train that were impossible to foresee. Whether one is thinking of human knowledge, or of human action, either complete knowledge, or completely predictable consequences to actions, are impossible. Life is, at the very least, surprising.

This has been noted by a lot of thinkers. In the twentieth century, Gödel's Proof[1] in mathematics has restated this truth with mathematical and logical rigor. Not being a mathematician, I can only restate the conclusion of Gödel, and accept its validity on the authority of more learned men than I. However, I have no trouble accepting and believing its conclusion. Briefly, Gödel proved that no mathematical system could be self-complete without an infinite number of axioms. Only an infinite system can be self-complete for exactly the above stated reasons. Each axiom that solves one problem generates several more, and will require several more

1. Van Heijenoort, "Gödel's Theorem," in *Encyclopedia of Philosophy*, 348–57.

axioms to solve each of those problems, which in turn generate more (or, a mathematical system can never be self-complete because insoluble questions can be asked it from a transcendent system).

The Absolute Idealists, a group of English and American philosophers at the end of the nineteenth century, and the beginning of the twentieth, made much of similar considerations. Every proposition is only intelligible as a part of a complete system of knowledge, and that entire system conditions to some degree, every single proposition. This is similar to the illustration often used by people interested in "chaos theory," that the fluttering of the wings of a butterfly on this side of the world will have incalculable effects on the weather systems of the other side of the world. The difficulty that the Absolute Idealists stubbed their toes over was the insight that unless one knew the entire system, one could not adequately know any single proposition either; to know the entire system would require omniscience.

Michael Polyani's more recent work has again re-emphasized the bottomless character of all knowledge. Polyani has noted that all knowledge is premised on prior "tacit" knowledge that one is almost never aware of. It is unconsciously presupposed. This is partly what makes teaching so difficult. The teacher passes on a surface of his knowledge, but does not realize all of the unspoken foundations that have made that particular knowledge coherent to him. Great masters in virtually any field can rarely give a credible account of how they do what they do. They do not know how they know what they know, or do what they do. Most of their knowledge is "tacit." Polyani uses Stradivarius, the great violinmaker, as an example. He was an unlearned man, and in fact illiterate, but, as everyone knows, a master craftsman. Nobody today knows how he did what he did. Stradivarius himself could probably have not verbally explained to anyone how he did it. He could teach and show apprentices, but this knowledge could never entirely be verbally transmitted.[2]

In its baldest form, this paradox has sometimes been stated in this epigram or axiom: "You can't know anything unless you know everything." The difficulty with this is that something is obviously wrong with it. If it were strictly true, then one could not know that the axiom itself was true. If it were strictly true, then the Absolute Idealists could never know their own theory, because presumably, none of them were omniscient. And indeed, this very consideration was one of the reasons that the Idealists were overthrown in their one time unquestioned intellectual reign. On the other

2. Polanyi, *Personal Knowledge*, 53.

hand, it is an axiom that is very difficult to unhinge. There is something right about it and something wrong about it. There is a hole somewhere in the middle of it. It seems intuitively the case that if knowledge is at all interconnected and systematic, then the entire system will affect every particular of it, and ignorance of the whole system will necessarily mean that what knowledge we do have is inaccurate at least to some degree, if not, in fact, fatally so. Is it possible that the only thing we know is that we know nothing? One must confess, this seems theoretically possible, but since everything is not known, it could never be known with certitude. And the paradoxes go on.

This no man's land in the realm of knowledge is something that the Bible has a great deal to say about. Man has determined to become his own god. Once he has done that, though, he is saddled with the fact that he is a pathetically inadequate god. He is now obligated to perform many of the functions of God, all by himself, when he simply lacks the requisite equipment to carry out the task. There is almost nothing worse in the workplace than putting someone in a position of responsibility over their head. To make an inexperienced worker a foreman before he is ready or experienced is a sure road to knots in the stomach, ulcers, nervous breakdowns, hives, and any of a million other psychosomatic difficulties. His body will tell him the truth, even if his pride will not own up. By eating presumptively and disobediently, Adam tried to make himself the origin of the knowledge of good and evil apart from God. He was ironically rewarded with just what he wanted, and mankind has ever since been saddled with the futility of being the origin of all knowledge, all of which has an ethical center. In this sense, the fall does have a "philosophical" core about it. If a child dresses up, and "plays judge," he isn't really a judge, because he doesn't know the law to interpret it. He has to play at knowing it, and pontificate and strut in "handing down decisions." He, in other words, has to "invent" the law, because in his minority, he is in no position to know it. Adam didn't know it, and refused to be a student. So he got thrust out, and had to keep "playing judge" in a grownup's world. The rest of history reads a little bit like William Golding's novel, *The Lord of the Flies*.[3]

The Bible tells us a good deal about God's knowledge. God knows everything. This is very helpful when you are God. When one is only a "god,"

---

3. The gist of the novel is a gibe at the notion of "the innocence of children." A group of children stranded on an island after a plane crash replicate all of the evils of the adult world. Golding, *Lord of the Flies*.

and one has even gone so far as to make the omniscient God one's enemy, one is in difficulty. For the sake of the Absolute Idealists, it is a very good thing that the God of the Bible does exist. For if he did not, the paradox that they struggle with ("in order to know anything, one must know everything") would not be only a puzzling paradox, but a flat contradiction that would in fact destroy all knowledge. For the gracious truth is that the God of the universe has not abandoned his naughty creatures who have insisted on being in charge. Behind the scenes, God is still guaranteeing the foundations of knowledge, even for those who deny his authority or even existence. At any time, God can rightfully call into question the lack of gratitude of those who presume on his foundation, but will not acknowledge it. Somewhere, there must be omniscience; otherwise, there is no reliable authority to believe the assumptions and foundations that all finite knowledge must begin with. Unless somebody reliable can assure us that unproven first principles on which all other knowledge is erected are true, then the rest of the temple of knowledge is simply fatuous. What if men were really turned over to their own assumptions of intellectual autonomy?

There are a lot of things simply taken for granted. For example, we take for granted, that the universe really is a system of coherent reality. But is it? How do we know such a thing? It is assumed that the laws of chemistry or of physics function exactly the same way on in a galaxy one hundred billion light years away as they do on earth. It is assumed that the laws governing atomic and hydrogen explosions function the same way on a far distant star as they do on our own sun and on our own earth. By what right do we assume such a thing, though? It is inconceivable that two plus two would equal anything but four in any place, known or unknown in the entire universe. Is this a justifiable assumption? Is there any place or any time where the law of contradiction could be suspended and opposites would equal each other, or is the law of contradiction necessary? That grass is green is apparently contingent, and could not be deduced necessarily beforehand from the mere laws of logic, but do we really know that this is not necessary? Do we know that the freezing point of water, or its boiling point is necessary, or not necessary? How do we know? Are the laws that we have in the universe haphazard or do they have to be and can be no other? Unless someone who knows everything assures us of the foundations, and tells us enough for us to be able to proceed with confidence, we do not know. With the Bible in hand, though, we do know.[4]

---

4. I touch on this issue of proceeding with confidence, briefly, in chapter 8 and chapter 9.

THE ONE AND THE MANY

Much can be made of the paradoxes of human knowledge that are transformed into contradictions when the God of the Bible is left out of our thinking. One of the most puzzling of paradoxes is the one/many problem. This is intuitively a very simple problem, and theoretically an impossible one for the naked human intellect. It quite simply means that our daily human experience has both a thread of unity while containing many elements of difference. For example, the room in which you are at the moment sitting is an obvious unity, or it would not be referred to as a "room." It is a "thing" that coheres as a single item. Yet, it contains many diverse things *at the same time*. That is a very simple reality, and it applies all the way from the reality of a single atom (which is one thing made up of many sub-atomic particles), all the way up to the complete dimensions of the whole universe (a single, albeit immense thing, made up of many, many lesser diverse things such as galaxies, stars, planets, moons, dust, etc.). As is often the case, though, the simplest things become the most puzzling when thought through.

In philosophical thought, this dilemma has expressed itself in numerous ways. In its most extreme form, there has been a flat denial of either the reality of any unity or of any diversity. Either unity or diversity is seen as illusion, and the deepest reality the opposite of what is denied. Eastern thought has tended to assert that diversity is illusory, and that reality is ultimately one. Western thought has tended to veer in the other direction, with a thinker like Hume almost denying any unity to the multitude of things at all.

The difficulty with an absolute position in these things is that if the deepest reality is either complete unity with no diversity, or complete diversity with no unity, then once again, the truth of this could never be either known or asserted. All knowledge, and all assertion require both elements at the same time. If everything were really and truly absolutely the same, there would be nothing to know, and nothing to think about. If everything were absolutely different with no handles of analogy or no coherence

---

The entire scientific enterprise, as well as everyday workable knowledge, depends on our foundations. Unitarian Islam produces an entirely different kind of world from trinitarian Christendom, and it is not a world that encourages curiosity, investigation, or discovery. Allah is a completely unknowable God. As a monad, He cannot know himself in any other person, and hence neither the world, nor finite persons can be known either. The Unitiarianism of Islam has all of the same problems as Aristotle's unmoved mover, and it leads to all of the same problems for the human knower that I discussed in chapter 1.

together, or if every item did not fit with every other item in some form of system, then again, there would be nothing to know or think about. As a result, most philosophers have tended not to an absolute position, but have contented themselves with theorizing that either unity or diversity is uppermost or paramount or original, with the other element being secondary and derivative. This seems very promising, but is fraught with difficulties. When one analyzes various perspectives that give priority to either unity or diversity, it seems impossible for that which is not prior to not dissolve under inspection into illusion or unreality.

The distressing habit of the human mind (apart from revelation) is to fall into dualisms. It does this so often, that one begins to believe that this is not accidental. It is in the nature of these dualisms that both sides of the dualism seem to demand the right to swallow the entire entity. Each half of the dualism considers itself the sole proprietor in every transaction, but has to put up with a hated business partner instead.

In Greek thought, the world is made up of two utterly unknowable opposites: form and matter. Form or matter, in their purest senses, are to the human mind, complete blanks. Pure form is without any distinction or differentiation whatsoever, and pure matter is without any unity or sameness whatsoever. The Greek hope is that if two unknowables are combined or added together, they will come together to make knowledge possible. The question is whether the Greek solution is like salt, in which two deadly poisons as elements combine to form a useful compound, or whether it is rather like adding two zeros together that still add up to zero.

The great surprise is that when God revealed himself, he showed himself not in the form of one, or of two, but rather as a trinity. Historically, the choice has been between being swallowed (monism), an unstable stab at intelligibility (dualism), or an adequate stable foundation for everything (the Trinity).

One is back to the dilemma already understood in the ancient world. Change in our world is ultimately destructive. The Egyptian pyramid is the most fitting of all structures and symbols. The pyramid was built in defiance against the sands of the desert. If the good can ever be reached, then one wants to maintain it, forever. The sands represent the enemy of all that is good and true. They are ever shifting and without any shape and are the opposite of order. The pyramid defiantly stands in unchanging geometric perfection, forever.

The modern world, however, says "hope and change." Now how did modernity come to associate the good with change? That is against all of the assumptions of the ancient world. When Heraclites said that one cannot put one's foot in the same river twice, he was not complimenting the river. He was not giving us an ancient version of "variety is the spice of life." He was cursing the river and giving expression to ancient despair and even nihilism.

The single most telling point of Cochrane's volume, *Christianity and Classical Culture*, is that the ancient world, culminating in Caesar Augustus, could not cope with time and change. How ironic, or providential, that Jesus was born in the very time, even the very year of the *apogee*—of classical perfection in the reign of Caesar Augustus—the time when all human achievement had been tried and exhausted. The ideal of the Greek city-state, and further on, of the even the whole of the Roman Empire, was that one achieved the completeness of perfection in a state and personage (in the Caesar himself), and that one wanted to never veer from that achievement.[5] But alas! The pyramid does *not*, in fact, stand in eternal perfection. The sands will eventually overwhelm even that, and the pyramid will itself turn to shifting and formless sand. Heraclites was right.

Just as the Bible has its logos in the second person of the Trinity, so Heraclites had his own logos. He recognized that even his own statement of not stepping in the same river twice would be incomprehensible if there were not some other element at work. In common with most of ancient antiquity, he posited the abstraction of reason, the logos, from which we derive our English word, "logic." The logos must intercept the river at some point, it most hold it still, it must freeze it. Words do that, at least in an ideal way. How does the world of matter ever come into contact with the world of form or reason? If it does, is it a stable or unstable configuration? One desires to escape the world of matter, because while one may be able to construct the seemingly timeless pyramid there, it is not really timeless. Given enough time, the instantiation of the reasonable form on the unreasonable matter will come unglued. It will not stay. The ungluing process is

---

5. Another fitting analogy for the Classical world's view of perfection is sculpture or statuary. The sculpture captures the fleeting moment of beautiful form forever, never to change, This was also their political hope. They hoped that the moment of political perfection could be captured and frozen forever in the city-state or the Empire. But of course, it could not. Time marched on . . . to ruin. As Cochrane notes, Augustine's thought could deal with time and change. A thousand years of Classical thought never could. Cochrane, *Christianity and Classical Culture*, see chapter 12, "Divine Necessity and Human History," 456–516.

what worried the ancients. They saw too much of it. "A good thing never lasts" was exactly their sentiment, and it was borne out by much patient observation. They were not pessimists for nothing.

At this point, one has several alternatives. One can assume a thoroughgoing dualism that assumes a possible gluing process that is most unreliable. Or, one can assume what the civilizations further to the East commonly assumed—the mirage-like quality of the current world—and assert that the goal of life is to escape from so much miserable fantasy to a reality that is an eternal one. All is really one. The instantiation that the Greeks assumed was too delicate, too temporary, too hastily undone. It is better to assume the thoroughly illusory quality of it from the outset, and one must escape this world of illusion to a final oneness that has no flowing rivers into which one cannot step even twice, let alone enough to make a workable life. One escapes to everlasting permanence, everlasting form. For that form to be everlasting, though, it must be uncomplicated. It must be one, and no more than one. If all is one, it is no different from nothingness. The escape to oneness is the same as an escape to nothingness. The world of time is unreliable, so one must escape to the one or the nothing.

The ancient world tried to live by dualisms, and when it found that marriage intolerable, it sought solitude in a final monism. I am not sure that the ancient world was not, in the end, a hermit. Marriage was just too hard, or was illusory in the first place.

The ancients always had a difficult time giving limited, but appropriate place to most things. Most things and principles were either reviled or worshipped, with not much in between. The ancient world had little idea for what to do with woman. Many deities were feminine, but the feminine principle also received the lion's share of blame for all wrong in the world. Our word for "matter" was the Latin word for mother (*mater*). Matter was a feminine principle, but was also uncontainable and rebellious. Form was a masculine principle, and it imposed itself, or was imposed on shapeless matter (an idea not congenial to modern feminists), but matter could not be ultimately contained or shaped and was constantly breaking out into shapeless mass (no girdle could contain her).

As another example, there is a near impossibility of reconciling a lunar (female) calendar with a solar (masculine) calendar. The two principles do not have easy compatibility.[6] Likewise, tragedy was very much a literary ex-

6. The final triumph of the Gregorian calendar (1582) leading to the final modern calendar that we follow today was no mean achievement. It was only accomplished with

pression of this same impossibility and lack of harmony. In tragedy, which was the highest and final literary form in the ancient world, death has the final say. The curtain will finally go down, even on the greatest of heroes, in eternal darkness and chaos.

World-weariness and despair is what came of the world before Christ came into it. To attempt to understand the world, or reconcile it to itself from the inside is futile if the exertions of that world mean anything. She cannot be understood from the inside. She can only be explained from the outside. Christ came down from heaven to illumine all things. What he showed us was something that could only barely be guessed at, if at all. It is what we saw in the last chapter, unveiled for us in the prologue to John's gospel. What is behind everything is not one, and not two, but three. Beyond that, and beyond guess, it is all one at the same time.

Folk sayings aren't always right, or at least don't always apply in every situation. "Two's company but three's a crowd" is a marvelously true saying for young lovers, but is bad cosmology and bad metaphysics. It is, however a repetition of the cosmology of most of the ancient world. When the ancient world fell from honeymoon to the dreariness of day-to-day marital life, then metaphysically, she usually sought to repeat the old magic with paramours and mistresses, or sought solace in solitude.

It simply isn't true that in the long run "two is company." The most likely business arrangement to come to wreck is the business partnership between two partners. In the long run, the likelihood of a falling out and disagreement over how things should be done is just too high, and business experts tell me that the fatality rate for this sort of partnership is the highest of all business mortalities. Nor, upon closer examination is two in marriage ever really just two, when viewed more deeply. I am not suggesting polyandry or polygamy as a replacement. I am suggesting two is fine, but we need to understand the necessity of the third to bring the two together.

Years ago, Robert Capon published a very fine book on marriage called *Bed and Board*.[7] The suggestion of the title was that a third entity was necessary to make a success of the tandem. The marital bed and the

---

devices of leap years and various months with uneven numbers of days. The ancient world uniformly followed a lunar calendar. It was only with the coming of Christ (who is the great Sun in the Heavenly sky), that a solar calendar that harmonized with the lunar calendar became a final necessity. This is very much in concert with the prophesy in the last book of the Old Testament: "The Sun of Righteousness will arise with healing in his wings" (Mal 4:2).

7. Capon, *Bed and Board*.

dinner table introduced both connection and goodness (or generosity) into the equation. The bed makes possible physical communion, which begets children. The board introduces the communion of the meal together; it is the place of hospitality. If either the bed or the board do not have outflow, then the result is a Dead Sea effect. The marriage becomes a salt solution in which nothing can live and eventually suffocates even the couple themselves. The third is necessary for the life of the two. Three is not a crowd; it is a metaphysically necessary minimum for the survival and health of the two. All of this has its origin and explanation in the Trinity.

AND, FINALLY, PERICHORESIS

Some words just roll around in your mouth, and are fun to say. I have always felt that way about the word "ubiquitous" (look it up if you don't know what it means). Of course, the supreme example is "supercalifragilisticexpialidocious" from *Mary Poppins*, a word that was invented to be nothing but fun to say. Amongst the best words in the entire world, however, are "perichoresis" and "circuminsession," which, by an extraordinary stroke of providence, happen to mean approximately the same thing. They are words attached to Trinitarian theology, and they explain why life and knowledge are possible at all. Loosely translated, perichoresis means "a dance." The Holy Trinity is a dance of Father, Son, and Holy Spirit. Circuminsession means "interpenetration." When we say Father, Son, and Holy Spirit are three distinct persons all of one essence, it has some startling implications. In John 14:10, Jesus says, "I am in the Father, and the Father in me." Now, what this implies is that the Father and the Son wholly and completely interpenetrate one another. They wholly share the same essence. Later, Jesus says, "If anyone loves me, he will keep my word, and my Father will love him, and we will come to him and make our home with him" (John 14:23). The way the Father and the Son will come is in the person of the Holy Spirit, who, likewise, shares in this dance, this complete interpenetration. "However, when he, the Spirit of truth has come, he will glorify me, for he will take of what is mine and declare it to you. All things that the Father has are mine. Therefore I said that he will take of mine and declare it to you" (John 16:13–15).

This is awfully complex and profound, so for our purposes, I am only going to say a few very simple things about it. The Godhead, the Triune God, is a God who knows himself, and in Van Til's thought, knows himself exhaustively. For Van Til, there are no hidden or subconscious depths in God and he is exhaustively self-conscious.[8] He knows himself, *because* he knows himself interpersonally. Each person knows himself in the other Persons. The Father knows himself in the Son and the Spirit. The Spirit knows himself in the Father and the Son, and the Son knows himself in the Father and the Spirit.

Every form of Unitarianism—whether the English and American variety in Unitarian Universalism, or in Islam—prides itself on not being encumbered with irrational and difficult doctrines like the Trinity. But the Trinity, far from being "irrational" is the very basis of both knowledge and rationality. A Unitarian god who is a pure monad, cannot know himself. He has no one in which to know himself; he is the same as a blank.

This is comprehensible in our own human relationships. An infant first knows himself *in* and *through* his or her mother, and following along only slightly later, the father, and siblings. To give an illustration, when we are confused, or don't know quite what to think, we search out a friend, or a counselor, to "talk it over." It is in communion with another human being that knowledge dawns on us. This sort of knowledge has its origins in the perichoresis of the Trinity. We can only know ourselves in one another as persons. Behind that, however, what makes it possible in the first place is that God knows himself as three persons, who exhaustively interpenetrate each other. Ultimately, this is how we know ourselves, and anyone else around us. God is behind it, under it, and in it (back to the second chapter—"God speaks, therefore I am").[9]

All of human life is a reflection of this. I know myself *in* and *through* my wife, my children, my parents, and my friends. All of life is one vast

8. Van Til, *Defense*, 35–36; Rushdoony, *One and the Many*, 8.

9. Augustine was one of those rare thinkers whose every book was an earthquake, and changed the world. It is sometimes said that Augustine "invented" history in his great volume, *The City of God*. It would not be unfair to say that Augustine also "invented" personality. His *Confessions* are a self-revelation, and he comes to know himself in a book length interaction, prayer, to God. It is in God that Augustine comes to know Augustine. Compare Augustine's self-knowledge with Marcus Aurelius' *Meditations*, which by comparison, are wholly "impersonal." It is not that Marcus Aurelius is trying to be impersonal and hide from us. It is rather that personal revelation had never so much as occurred to him in the first place. He did not know the Triune God. He had no one in this comprehensive sense in which to know himself. Of course, God was still there, and the very fact that an ancient man could so much as tell us his own name indicates that "the Light was shining" (i.e., God was there in the background). However, a full and personal revelation was not yet given in the pagan world. Were it otherwise, no pagan could have put two words, let alone two sentences, together.

conversation, and to be able to "talk" on the deepest level is the highest form of human existence.[10] Marital intercourse is a physical act fraught with more symbolic overlay of interpersonal communion than any other, and is perhaps closer to Trinitarian interpenetration than any other. In the Bible, it will often say so and so "knew" his wife, meaning intercourse. This is also why solitary confinement is the very worst punishment that can be inflicted on prisoners. Knowledge and consciousness are interpersonal; all of society is a finite analogue or replica of the inner life of God, and ultimately depends on him. The blessed Trinity is the foundation of all light, understanding, and knowledge.

FROM THE WESTMINSTER CONFESSION OF FAITH (1646)

> In the unity of the Godhead there be three Persons of one substance, power, and eternity: God the Father, God the Son, and God the Holy Ghost. The Father is of none, neither begotten nor proceeding; the Son is eternally begotten of the Father; the Holy Ghost eternally proceeding from the Father and the Son.[11]

The created order is an *analogue* to the Triune God, who is the source of this order and comprehensibility. The world is *one*, but it is at the same time *many*, and all things within the creation are *related* to one another, in various parallel and hierarchical ways, by the will of God. The law of identity (a = a), is just as ultimate as the law of contradiction (a does not = b), and neither is more fundamental. Each person within the Trinity is distinct. The Father is not the Son, the Son is not the Holy Spirit, the Holy Spirit is not the Father or the Son. Yet, the Father, Son and Holy Spirit are all three of one substance. Further, when God created, the Father created *through* the Son, *by means* of the Holy Spirit.[12] Unlike the God of Aristotle, or the God

---

10. It is also the case that not only do I know the creation below me as "things" and "facts" because they contain and are constructed by the Word and grammar of God, but I also know myself and other persons and even God in these "facts" and "things." Because of the grammar in them, I carry on a conversation with them, and I know myself and others and even God "in" them. This is the very foundation of metaphor and poetry. The whole universe participates in a kind of creaturely perichoresis as an analogy to trinitarian perichoresis. Leithart, *Deep Comedy*, 73–95.

11. Schaff, *Creeds of Christendom*, 3:606.

12. This is a bare introduction to the profundities of trinitarian theology. I briefly refer the reader back to the previous chapter's exegesis of John 1:1. See also St. Augustine's *De Trinitate*, which is available in many places, including free electronic downloads. Like

of Islam (the Unmoved Mover, and Allah) the God of the Bible knows *you*. He knows the smallest detail of your life—he knows every hair on your head, and every bird that falls from the sky (Matt 10:29–31)—and he also knows exactly how and where you fit in the entire vast and comprehensive *system* of the whole universe and all of heaven and hell as well.[13] Aristotle's God is incapable of knowing anything about you other than the fact that you belong to the genus called "humanity" (whatever that is with no individuality). It is entirely unclear if Allah knows even that much about you. However, the God of Abraham, Isaac, and Jacob; the God of Jesus Christ, is both closer to you and more intimate with you than your own left hand, an old and familiar shoe, or your beloved puppy dog (and he is so humble that he does not eschew the comparisons). At the same time, he is more high and lifted up than all of the stars and galaxies combined. And you don't want to make his acquaintance?

---

all of what Augustine wrote (that most personal of all of the Fathers), is most accessible. Augustine, "On the Holy Trinity."

13. "For I am God . . . declaring the end from the beginning" (Isa 46:9–10); "I am the First and the Last" (Rev 1:17).

7

The Proofs

ANSELM

IN THE HISTORY OF the world, many people have written books in order to make a contribution, to be remembered, or even in order to become famous. Only a few people have been so privileged to have not written whole books, but only a few stunning and amazing paragraphs. Abraham Lincoln, for example, is today remembered for the several paragraphs of the Second Inaugural Address, and the Gettysburg Address. A friend of mine, in reference to the Second Inaugural Address, said, "Nobody can write like that today," and I think he is right. These are masterpiece paragraphs more worthy than many long books, and the condensed result of far more sweat and blood than many volumes.

Another gentleman who authored four remarkably memorable paragraphs was a man named Anselm (at least these paragraphs are remembered from a short book). Anselm was a bishop in the English church during the eleventh century. His four short paragraphs constitute his own proof for the existence of God.

If you will have the patience to sit and stare and think about these paragraphs for a while, you can reduplicate in yourself all of the same feelings that deep thinkers have had about them for hundreds of years. It is like staring at those computer-generated squiggle pictures. If you look the right way, it all comes into amazing three-dimensional focus. You're not sure if you have been given the open sesame to the cosmos, the universal answer to the sphinx's riddle, or if Anselm is only a philosophic used car salesman peddling a worthless optical illusion. The thing is either maddening or ecstatically delightful, depending on what you are looking for. To further set you up for it, let me give you this teaser. All of human life bears about with it at least a seed of pessimism. All ancient civilizations, and especially civilizations of the east, bear the character of fatalism. The fear that the gods would envy anyone's good luck is a very deeply felt sentiment, even among those of us who are not superstitious. There is an old saying that arises from the generally disappointing character of human life: "It is too good to be true." Everybody knows what this means, because everybody has been disappointed. It's best not to get your hopes up too high, because you merely set yourself up for a great let down.

Great thinking often carries a great surprise within it. It turns everything on its head and it reverses all of our previously held prejudices. Anselm's "ontological proof" is a wonderful demonstration of this. The ontological proof takes the axiom, "It is too good to be true," and claims to demonstrate precisely that in the highest case possible, if it is too good to be true, then this is the very proof that it is. In fact, it is not just perhaps true, or quite possibly true, but it is infallibly and necessarily true. The existence of God is the highest instance of this feeling, and Anselm claims that the felt sentiment that "God's existence is too good to be true," is in fact the very proof of the fact that he does. To even be able to conceive of God's greatness, according to Anselm, proves that he exists. Here is his proof:

> And so, Lord, do Thou, who dost give understanding to faith, give to me so far as Thou knowest it to be profitable, to understand that Thou art as we believe; and that Thou art that which we believe. And indeed, we believe that Thou art a being than which nothing greater can be conceived. Or is there no such nature, since the fool hath said in his heart, there is no god? (Ps 14:1) But at any rate, this very fool, when he hears of this being of which I speak—a being than which nothing greater can be conceived—understands what he hears, and what he understands is in his understanding; although he does not understand it to exist.
>
> For, it is one thing for an object to be in the understanding, and another to understand that the object exists. When a painter first conceives of what he will afterwards perform, he has it in his understanding, but he does not yet understand it to be, because he has not yet performed it. But after he has made the painting, he both has it in his understanding, and he understands that it exists, because he has made it.
>
> Hence, even the fool is convinced that something exists in the understanding, at least, which nothing greater can be conceived. For when he hears of this he understands it. And whatever is understood, exists in the understanding. And assuredly that,

than which nothing greater can be conceived, cannot exist in the understanding alone. For suppose it exists in the understanding alone: then it can be conceived to exist in reality; which is greater.

Therefore, if that, than which nothing greater can be conceived, exists in the understanding alone, the very being, than which nothing greater can be conceived, is one, than which a greater can be conceived. But obviously this is impossible. Hence, there is no doubt that there exists a being, than which nothing greater can be conceived, and it exists both in the understanding and in reality.[1]

There it is in all of its brief, maddening, beauty. Does it work? There are a few difficulties attending upon it that need to be examined.

Conception is different from imagination. I can *conceive* of many things that I cannot *imagine*. Imagination is often (but not always) tied to sense experience, and many things are intellectually available that are not pictorially seeable, or cannot be tasted, touched, heard, or smelled. The severe abstractions of almost all modern physics, and of higher mathematics are examples of this. The very puzzling nature of these disciplines is owing to the complete lack of any way to depict their meaning through senses. This is not a new reality. Plato understood this very well in the simplest terms. He posited that the senses owed their intelligibility to the forms, but that the forms themselves could not be pictured or imagined. Much of what makes Plato entertaining and delightful to young students is his capacity to demonstrate this very reality over and over in perplexing and fascinating ways. The equation 2+2=4 is an expression of pure arithmetic that is prior to any visible example of it, such as putting two sets of two blocks together, and counting the result as four blocks. The truth of 2+2=4 in no way depends upon the blocks, but rather the blocks in some way participate in a higher intellectual truth that is independent of any sensory demonstration.

Likewise, it may be impossible to *imagine* the greatness or perfection of God, but still possible to *conceive* of its reality. Or, to put it a different way, it may be possible to know *that* certain things are true of God, but know very little in regard to *what* the content of the "thatness" would be. In the case of God, however, this leaves us with certain difficulties that we do not have in regard to 2+2. *That* God has an identity and a character may be one thing, but it is surely no trivial thing to know *what* the character of perfection and greatness is, so that God can be known and identified.

1. Daniel, "Anselm's Ontological Argument."

It may be that concepts like "perfection" and "infinite greatness" do have some minimal usefulness when conceived of independently of revelation. A few days ago, I read something interesting about dogs and silk worms: Dogs, we are told, have a sense of smell *a million* times greater than their human masters. Likewise, by the sense of smell, a silk worm can detect the presence of a worm of the opposite sex from as far away as seven miles. There is no doubt that in this there is a certain kind of real, albeit very minimal and very formal knowledge. What on earth is the actual experience of smell a million times as powerful as ours? A whole world is closed to us by not experiencing that. We can deduce the reality of these things mathematically by counting numbers of necessary molecules needed to be present for detection, and we can fiddle with numbers, but the real and lived experience of the dog is a perfect mystery to us. It is essentially empty. I do not want to dishonor God by comparing him to a dog, but the comparison serves a useful purpose. The purely formal conception of "a being greater than which one cannot conceive" has a certain meaning, but it is extremely limited and formal, and very liable to corruption. As John Calvin said, the mind of man is a "factory of idols." The God of this conception is really, as perfection goes, almost perfectly unknown, and perhaps unknowable. A philosopher who set out to conceive of a being so great that a greater could not be conceived could hardly do more than assert the bare reality of such greatness. In all likelihood, he would only establish a false idol in his own intellect, insofar as he supplied content to the concept. For the darkness of the human mind is so great that such an enterprise would be doomed from the outset. How could he adequately establish and prove his notion of "greatness" and "perfection?"

This is one of the greatest difficulties attending the argument. Just who is this God of which no greater can be conceived? A running history of the commentary on the argument shows that in fact, different thinkers have thought that he (she or it) have quite different identities. Some form of this argument has been used since Plato, and philosophers of a rationalistic bent have very commonly turned to some version of it to prove that a real extra-mental perfection, or God, must exist. But he (she or it) could be any variety of different candidates. He (she or it) could be a pantheistic being, or the God of Aristotle, or of Islam, or of Christianity, or an unknown and unidentified God.

This is not where Anselm begins, however. He did not begin with a sheer rational deduction. Rather, he began with a prayer and it was a prayer to the God of the Bible, the God of the Christian confession. He prays to the God of Jesus Christ, who Anselm believed was the clear revelation of an otherwise very dimly known God. Anselm asks that God would affirm himself to be true, that which he as a Christian had already confessed ("And so, Lord, do Thou, who dost give understanding to faith, give to me so far as Thou knowest it to be profitable, to understand . . ."). Anselm then asserts that which Christian dogmatics believe about the being of God, the one who is the implication of all perfection, the one of whom it is impossible to even conceive of a greater: " . . .that Thou art as we believe; and that Thou art that which we believe. And indeed, we believe that Thou art a being than which nothing greater can be conceived." Anselm prays that the contents of what the Bible reveals as greatness above which it is impossible to conceive of rising, would be proven as true and existent.

How is God going to answer Anselm's prayer? By the way, Anselm asserts that this proof was indeed given to him in explicit answer to prayer. Anselm's prayer in the proof proper is not just a rhetorical device. The answer that came was in the nature of a negative proof, a proof from the absurdity of the contrary. Anselm imagines the position of the non-believer, the "fool." When he examines the position of the man who denies the truth of the Christian confession, the result is complete contradiction. It is not, Anselm discovers, possible to deny God's real extra-mental existence, and not bring human thought to a complete collapse.

Anselm is speaking as a Christian bishop whose vocation is to help fools to be healed of their folly. Or one could say he is speaking as an evangelist, or a pastor. This is very important to understand. This is usually referred to as "the ontological proof," but I think it could more accurately be termed "the proof from preaching," or "the proof from pastoral exhortation." He does not begin with a natural or intellectually neutral proof for God's existence. He does not begin with a general idea of God that may be innate or generated in just anybody's consciousness. He begins with preaching that is heard from the Bible, and in this he assumes the complete truth of the Christian Faith. Anselm is asserting that the act of the preaching of the gospel, and of the proclamation the God of the Bible *necessarily* implies his existence. Or one could say that the *word* of God (the Bible) necessarily implies the *existence* of God, because the Bible as the written word, which reveals Jesus Christ as the incarnate Word, reveals and manifests God's greatness and perfection. It is the revelation of one so great that a greater cannot be conceived. If the word of God illumined in the mind does not necessarily imply God's existence, then all of human conceptual power will explode in a train wreck because of the inherent contradiction that follows. Even a fool (a non-believer) can comprehend this contradiction. Fools are, by definition, not quick. Or if they are quick, they are perverse. This is why a bishop is necessary. The purpose of the bishop (in this case, Anselm) is to point out the contradiction to the fool, and press it in on him. He needs to have his attention forcefully called to the implications that are at hand. Otherwise, he will refuse to notice the real point. Or, since he is so slow on the draw, they will whiz right past him. So Anselm presses the point and says, "God is absolutely, comprehensibly perfect, and it would be a contradiction for this perfection to not include real existence." This turns things everything on its head. Once even the *idea* of the Pearl of Great Price[2] is found, and one in fearfulness says, "It is too good to be true," then Anselm's counsel is to immediately sell everything you have, and have your money in hand to make the purchase, because assuredly the "real thing" exists and will be up for sale. The one so conceived in the mind is one from whom truth overflows, and pours out. He is the cup of truth itself. He overflows with such overwhelming superabundance that it is impossible that he does not exist. God's being is so rich that even being conceived of in the mind necessitates his existence.

This is stating the issue positively. If we state it negatively, the man who doubts God's reality is a "fool" because he now has no grounds for even his own consciousness or for thinking inside of that consciousness. Part of the implication of this perfect God is that he created everything, including the hearer of the preaching. If he does not exist, then he has also not created. If nothing has been created, then the hearer also has not been created and does not exist. His thinking is a complete contradiction at this point, (which is foundational) and there is no other point where it can issue in truth or reality either, because it is to this God that this man owes his existence, his consciousness, and his capacity to think. A contradiction can issue in everything and nothing. This contradiction is so all-embracing that only "nothing" is left.

One other objection must be dealt with that has persistently come up: mental conception does not imply existence. They are different categories. The earliest objector used the example of conceiving of a most perfect

---

2. This is an allusion to one of Jesus' parables. "Again, the kingdom of heaven is like unto a merchant man seeking goodly pearls: Who when he had found one pearl of great price, went and sold all that he had, and bought it" (Matt 13:45–46).

island. Just because I conceive of it does not imply its existence, and this of course is true. But this is silly. God is *sui generis*; he is unique. Only God is the implication of *all* perfections. A most perfect island, or most perfect anything else is still not in any sense necessary as a result of the conceived perfections. Necessary existence (God could not, *not* exist) is only the case if he is the one who contains and is *all* perfections. *All* perfections would include existence as well.

The philosopher Kant also had problems with the proof. He thought that existence added nothing to the definition of a thing. He said that this wasn't how definitions worked. But surely this is fantastic. Only Kant could have said such a thing. One is tempted to think that in this instance, we have in Kant a "Freudian slip." I wonder if Kant disliked Anselm's proof because here, in one instance of reality, we have a case of "thinking makes it so." The difficulty is that for Anselm, this is true in only *one* instance. For Kant, oddly, it is in a sense true in all instances, but here, this becomes his objection. As a result, when he stubs his toe on the real thing, he must deny it, because the reality of his thinking everywhere else is too painfully absurd to admit. Is Kant living in denial, and does Anselm expose this? I wonder. It is hard to believe that even Kant *really* believed his own objection, and it shows his mentalized view of the world. He leaves one in the position of saying that there is no difference between unicorns, fairies, pumpkin coaches drawn by magical mice, and my wife, dog, and children sitting here in the same room with me, as long as I have an adequate definition of all of these things. If I said afterwards, "Oh by the way, the difference between a pumpkin coach drawn by magical mice and my wife is that she *exists*," this is surely at least a little bit significant. Existence adds *nothing*? That is an idealist proposition if ever I heard one, and I direct you to the comments below concerning that branch of philosophy. Would it have been just as good for Columbus to have *thought* about discovering a new world as opposed to actually doing it? Was the actual achievement of landing on the moon no better than millennia of men dreaming of doing it? If existence adds nothing, then this is the necessary consequence.

What of other candidates for the position of God besides the God of the Bible? Assuredly, contained in the very idea of God is the reality that there can only be one of him. It is impossible that there be two, three, or six Gods, because if there is someone else who is his equal, than it is possible to conceive of one greater than that one who has an equal. Let me briefly suggest, there are no other candidates. In no other place is there a revelation of *who* God is beyond *that* he exists. In no other place is there a God who can identify and know himself with absolute comprehensiveness. To be sure, I have not examined every other possibility. However, everywhere else that I am aware of outside of the Bible and outside of Jesus Christ, "God" is an empty formality. This would be true of philosophers from Plato and Aristotle, all the way through Hegel and beyond. It would be true of eastern monisms, and it would even be true of Islam. This is stating it negatively. To state it positively, I can only repeat what the author of the epistle to the Hebrews said, "God, who at various times and in various ways spoke in time past to the fathers by the prophets, has in these last days spoken to us by his Son." He cannot be superseded. He is the last and the only adequate word. He is known by tasting. He bids you come and see.

AQUINAS

Much is made in modern writing of how depressing the world is, because modern men have "lost God," and that is certainly true. A corollary to this, however, which is not as broadly perceived, is that the loss of the external and "real" world is just as depressing and just as catastrophic. If you shut a generation up inside of themselves for long enough, and they are very likely to begin to think that suicide is a preferable alternative. If we begin with human thought, and human perception, and then critique human thought and human perception, we can never get to external reality. A few modern thinkers have understood this very profoundly. Through the twentieth century, there was a great renewal in Thomistic thought. Among the principal figures of this revival were were Jacques Maritain (1882–1973), Etienne Gilson (1884–1978), and G. K. Chesterton himself (1874–1936). These kinds of thinkers do not like beginning with thought and ideas because they have a deep intuition of claustrophobia. They have noted that the head is a very small and cramped place, and not a comfortable place to be forced to live in. They like doors and windows, and like very much to get outside to the fresh air. They fear, more than anything, a head without windows, and conceive of it as a kind of prison. They have noted the insanity of many modern thinkers since Descartes who have gone mad in such small confines. They have been right about the mental *tendencies* of Descartes, Kant, Hegel, and even the Phenomenologists, and most other modern thinkers. They are all afflicted with Descartes' conceit concerning the vaunted (and illusory) creative powers of their own thought. They never do get out of their own heads to a reality outside of themselves, so of course they all tend to solipsism and craziness.[3]

These thinkers want to begin not with thought (as did Descartes), but rather, with what they term "an intuition of being," that is with the immediate intuition presented to the thinking and perceiving man of the existence of the world, and of existing objects outside of oneself. They maintain (quite sensibly) that modern thought that begins with perception and thought make, as an ideal, a "critique of thought" before there is anything to be thought about. They maintain that in that case, the mind begins with itself, and ends with itself. They are involved in a kind of philosophic anorexia, in which the brain feeds off of itself. Or, to use another illustration, this kind of modern thought is the opposite of casting a stone into a still pond, and watching a series of ever-growing concentric circles ripple outward from where the stone was thrown. The circles instead go inward, each smaller than the last.

We saw this in Descartes, and Descartes begins what is typical of what might be termed "mainstream" modern philosophic thought. This tendency continues and develops, ironically as philosophy tries to move forward. There is an increasing *desire* for growing outward concentric circles to more adequately deal with real human experience, but instead every effort acts like a boa constrictor creating tighter and tighter circles of starvation of the human mind and senses. This is especially true in the German philosophical giant, Immanuel Kant. He is very keen concerning experience, by which he means the exercise of our senses, as well as our minds, and of our sense of the beautiful, and in this he tries to go beyond Descartes, Hume, and Rousseau. For Kant, however, all experience is a result of our own minds imposing order on the "buzzing, blooming, confusion," and he never reaches the "outside." He maintains that this is impossible. An "unconditioned" experience cannot happen.

Against this, a powerful minority voice has been raised by a number of very able followers of the greatest of all of the medieval thinkers: Thomas Aquinas. These thinkers all have a powerful sense of the constricted nature and futility of "modernity." They recognize that the root of this constrictedness is modern self-centeredness. Modern thought is almost all a species of philosophic narcissism. Thought, they insist, cannot begin by examining itself; rather, it has to begin by thinking. In order to think, it has to have something to think about. Philosophy, they say, begins with intellect immediately apprehending being outside of itself. If intellect is not nourished by

3. Maritain, *Distinguish to Unite*.

"being" and the apprehension of the essences of being, then it has nothing to do. All of Kant's immense labors in his massive *Critique of Pure Reason* are really epistemological introvertedness, and his book could perhaps be more justly titled, *An Inspection of Pure Introspection.* Kant's effort is like taking out one's eyes to examine them. You can't both look at a thing, and think about looking at a thing at the same time. But Kant tries, and loses the reality of the thing at the very outset.

Ludwig Wittgenstein's famous dictum concerning philosophy being like being a fly inside of a bottle, buzzing about, trying to find a way out, and being unable to, is exactly apt to the situation. One has the feeling that Wittgenstein's near lifelong madness and struggle against suicide was not for garden-variety reasons (a love affair gone bad, money problems, etc.) but precisely because he felt the real tendencies towards complete claustrophobia in modern thought.

Personally, I can remember always having the sense, all the way back to college philosophy, that idealism *does* lead to solipsism. Although there were always violent objections to this as the outcome, I could never see how. Kantianism is never able to give a coherent account of how or why there is more than one mind or of how they all perceive in the same way. Identity or similarity is a category of the mind itself. Hence, I have (from a Kantian perspective) no way of knowing that the existence of other minds is anything other than a form imposed on whatever is out there *by me* and me alone. Of course, Kant wrote the *Critique of Pure Reason* with the *assumption* that other minds will perceive it.

G. K. Chesterton, the great English journalist, and surely one of the most sensible men of the twentieth century, is another example with a happier ending. To paraphrase his own deliberations, he asked an important question concerning modern thought: Are we dealing with external reality at all, or only with gyrations of the Kantianized brain that seeks internal coherence without any real reference to external being? Chesterton completely grasped the modern sickness of being unable to have a real world. In his early adult years, he experienced several years of near-suicidal depression. The cause of it was precisely the sense of being a "fly in the bottle." One can entirely sympathize with the reasons for Chesterton's years of melancholy and despair as a young man. He was depressed because he despaired of ever escaping the enclosed and encapsulated self for the "real world" or "real things." The gravity was too great, and the escape velocity of Kantianism was too slow. He eventually became a Thomist because he grasped that the self and the mind need "real things" to nourish real thought. In German "ideosophy" (as some of the Thomists call "modern" thought) we have nothing but selfist inversion. Chesterton was clear that for him, the enemy was not materialism, but solipsism, or selfism. If one *begins* with perception and then moves to the *critique* of perception, one never escapes to any*thing* to be thought about. Part of what helped him (after which he became the most cheerful of men) was his discovery of the Thomist doctrine of "the intuition of being." He was able to get outside of himself, and beyond that, even further. Chesterton discovered that there was an implication to the existence of the world, and like our previous section, it is an implication that is good beyond imagination. Eventually, Chesterton found his way home; he became a believing Christian.

THE FIVE PROOFS

Thomas Aquinas, of course, developed five proofs for the existence of God. They all reason from the "common sense" facts of the world to the reality of God. They include reasoning from the everyday experiences of, causality, motion, design, and morality. He takes note of our sense of the "contingency" of the world and everything in it. That means, quite simply, our sense of its non-necessity, dependence, and incompleteness.

After all these centuries of the proofs being as set forth by Thomas and those following (he put them forth in the thirteenth century), the results seem to be ambiguous, and even disappointing. Some would say that Thomas never generated his arguments in the first place to persuade unbelievers, but rather wrote them to confirm the faithful in what they already knew. This is possible, but the proofs have always been used to attempt to persuade the non-persuaded. However, my experience would indicate that generally speaking amongst unbelievers, the man on the street is loosely unconvinced, the philosopher is rigorously unconvinced, and the Christian is confirmed in what he already knows. The believer is strongly tempted to false optimism, hoping he can get his unbelieving neighbor to see what he sees. It seems this rarely happens.

Two of the wisest Catholic apologists, one of them a passionate Thomist, have said as much, either by direct confession, or by what isn't said. Pascal, the renowned seventeenth century mathematician, says the proofs are virtually worthless for the purposes of convincing non-believers to bend the knee in submission.[4] Chesterton, who was very devoted to Thomas and many of his doctrines, never says a word about the proofs. Indeed, it is perhaps telling that Chesterton would write an entire book on Thomas Aquinas, and only in an indirect and circular way say anything about the proofs. [5]

In *Orthodoxy,* which is virtually Chesterton's spiritual autobiography, it is clear that the proofs had nothing to do with his conversion at all.[6] Jacques Maritain, one of the most brilliant of modern Thomists, came to the proofs as a further witness to what he already believed. He and his wife were drawn to faith by the life that they saw incarnated in various Christians who they came to know.[7]

Rather, one seems to get out of the proofs what one puts into them. If I am already a Christian, then nothing is more sensible then to see in the intricate design of the world, in the reality of moral conscience, and in the contingency of all things, the very direct hand of God. If I am not a believer, these realities are hidden from me, and in many cases, there is violent opposition to God as the conclusion of these arguments. They perhaps work for Christians because they bring other knowledge and data to the table than what is baldly stated in the propositions themselves. They perhaps don't work for non-Christians, because they, too, bring auxiliary

4. Pascal, *Pensees*, 781.

5. Chesterton, *Saint Thomas Aquinas.*

6. This continues to amaze me, and I never see anyone comment on it. It seems to have been irrelevant to Chesterton. What was relevant to him was at heart, Thomas' "intuition of being"; translated, Thomas' beginning with the reality of creation. It enabled him to escape his own sense of cursed autonomy, which left him with a de-facto solipsism. Chesterton argued in a non-vicious circle. One begins with creation and ends with the God of the Bible. If one takes Chesterton altogether in his greatest writings (on Thomas and Francis, *Orthodoxy*, *Everlasting Man*, and *The Ball and the Cross*, and *The Man Who Was Thursday*) one essentially finds pre-suppositionalism with literary genius. In *Orthodoxy*, which is his most extended and complete apologetic, his argument is all a *reductio*; to not believe reduces one to absurdity, and only *Orthodoxy* can give one the necessary preconditions to know, or to act. He hated modern egoism, pluralism ("the world nearly died of broad mindedness once before"), and new age pantheism (the ball is the symbol of all pantheisms, ancient and modern—the Cross brings the crisis of the Living God). *The Man Who Was Thursday* is (beyond a doubt!) the greatest novel of the twentieth century. It premises that all Christians are secret agents who are blowing up the modern world, and, at the same time, secret agents who are establishing the new rule and order of God. Chesterton got there in regard to Thomas and almost everything else, years before anyone else.

7. Maritain, *We Have Been Friends.*

assumptions to the table that are often unstated. Christians already know that the world is the creation of God. Non-Christians already know that whatever the world is, the explanation has to be something other than the God of the Bible. They know that, in some way, the facts simply are there, and somehow the world is self-contained. Indeed the proofs, as they stand, are a species of induction, and it is well known that induction can never lead to certain conclusions. At best, they lead to probable conclusions, and if it is only probable that God exists, then there is always also a chance that he doesn't exist, and that an alternative explanation is possible. Experience teaches that if there is *any* wiggle room at all, it will be used to wiggle out of the reality of God's existence. The argument, for both Christians and non-Christians, is not really inductive at all. It is deductive; it is presuppositional. The non-Christian knows ahead of time that the universe is all there is, and the Christian knows ahead of time that the world is the creation of God that gives testimony to his creating hand everywhere.

What if we have gotten something backwards? A holier man than Thomas has never lived, and holiness gives people shrewdness of the sort that the common take on the proofs denies him. He is made out to be an intellectual out of touch with what might really persuade people in an ordinary way. What if Thomas was, in fact, going at things quite differently than we have been led to believe? Chesterton opens me to this possibility. How he could have written a masterpiece, and hardly uttered a word about the proofs? How can this be? He is, if anyone is, a "natural Thomist." No one has more natural sympathy with Thomas Aquinas than he. It is clear that he saw and understood something that Thomists who really belong to the inner clique have always gotten: Thomism is, at heart, about *things* in the most concrete kind of way. They have a kind of affection for things, and for real being that other, less cerebral, people reserve for their pets. They love things, and they love the world and the universe as a place of many, many things that can all be seen, praised, and held in awe.

Let me demonstrate my point by quoting another Thomist, Jacques Maritain:

> A hidden but powerful teleological motivation also intervenes at this point, to which idealism unconsciously obeys, so cheating at its own game. Idealism's concern is precisely that it not be led to a certain terminus; it aims to avoid a certain final conclusion. Now if, from the very start, things and the extramental stability whereby they regulate our thought are so carefully rejected, it is because of the fact, above all else, that owing to a secret instinct

that is the more imperious in that it remains unconfessed, the mind does not want in the end to be forced to come face to face with a transcendent, supreme reality, an abyss of personality before which our thought has to adore. The bastions and fortresses of idealistic philosophy thus appear to be just so many vast defense works against divine personality. Nothing is more significant than those far-flung works. It is enough that things exist for God to be unavoidable. Let us but grant to a bit of moss or the smallest ant its due nature as an ontological reality, and we can no longer escape the terrifying hand that made us.[8]

This is exactly the spirit of Thomas Aquinas; this is Thomism of the heart. There is an argument in this that could be reduced to a syllogism. Although I am aware that Thomism formally and technically argues from natural reason to God's existence, let me suggest that the following is the underlying, most basic, and first argument that Thomas and his greatest followers have always used.[9] It is simply this:

The world and all of the facts and things of the world are creatures.

All creatures are created by the God of Abraham, Isaac, and Jacob.

Therefore, the God of Abraham, Isaac, and Jacob, created the world and all of the facts and things of the world.

8. Maritain, *Distinguish to Unite*, 109.

9. Thomism, in spite of the fact that it has produced wonderful and liberating scholarship into this century, has an ambiguity right in the heart of it. Thomism is double minded. On the one hand, it wants to begin perception and thought with mere being instead of created being. On the other hand, I would suggest that it has not been true to itself, because nobody has a deeper real attachment to the world as a creation than Thomists. Nobody loves the world in a holy and sanctified way more than them. When they start from a "neutral" starting point, and then want to be able to find its way to God, they are doing a questionable thing. When one reads Thomas and his disciples, they want to use a "blockhouse methodology," to quote Van Til. That is, they want to build the first story of the building on the basis of natural reason, and proceed from there to reason their way to revelation. Reason can do so much all by itself, and it can then justify revelation. It is like a ladder that one can use to climb to the second story, which is the Bible. Reason is used to justify revelation. However, it is clear when one reads the really great Thomists, that really, they equivocate here. I doubt that Thomas ever regarded things as just things, purely to be apprehended by the naked intellect, any more than he would regard his mother as just some woman to be addressed in the third person. More than any other philosophers, the Thomists regard the world, with exceeding great love and affection. They regard the world as a creature. This is true of Thomas as much as it is St. Francis.

This is reasoning from creature to the Creator. It is the naive reasoning of a Christian. It is a full circle. The reality of God is wholly contained in the preceding idea of creation. If this is so, we are back to the very circle mentioned above. Don't Thomists want to speak to people who are outside of their club? So how have we gotten anywhere? But patience. Let's continue and see where this takes us.

Let's turn for a moment to Thomas Aquinas himself. I want to pare things down and get right to the nub: St. Thomas lived a long time ago, and he was fat. These are the two most relevant facts for us to deal with in regards to him. This is valuable information to us, because as it turns out, a long time ago, people were troubled by many of the same things that we are now. This surprises us, but it is good for us to learn; it shocks us out of our conceit, and invites us into the company of suffering humanity. There is no surer way to insulate yourself from cure for your troubles than to continually reassure yourself that "no one has ever suffered as I." This conceited sense of uniqueness is deadly, and modern people are full of this poison. There is a second kind of conceit that is exactly the opposite, but which stands as the inevitable companion to the first: folks exactly like me have always peopled the world. A politicized upper middle class American, may be completely sure that every tribesman and every third world peasant has always had his own sensibilities, his own sense of justice and equality, and his own outrage at all of the same wrongs. He regards himself as being universal in outlook, when in fact he is completely ethnocentric. It also turns out that although surprising sufferings and analogies are shared with many other people of different places and different times, people have also been shockingly dis-analogous to us. It never occurred to them what we take for granted.

St. Thomas was also fat, and since he was fat, he needed a very firm place in which to stand. God made him fat so he would have to find an adequate place to stand. In regard to this, he made a very stunning discovery. He discovered the world.[10] He was the Christopher Columbus of the world itself. The discovery was so amazing, and was so certain, that he set out with his new found knowledge to show its most certain implication: the very existence of God. Thomas was like the first man to wake up and discover

10. What convinced me years ago that Chesterton was a genius and not just a man of ability was the first chapter in *The Dumb Ox*, comparing St. Francis and St. Thomas (On Two Friars), and showing that they were both doing exactly the same thing, in spite of the black and white differences in temperament, calling, and gifts. Both were called by God to awaken the world to the being of the world. Francis' poem, "Brother Sun, Sister Moon" is very much the real spirit of Thomas as well. Chesterton, *Saint Thomas Aquinas,* 19–48.

that the sun shined. Nobody before him had ever noticed. Of course, it had been shining all along, but somebody first noted the fact. It is remarkable to notice these things. Thomas didn't *demonstrate* that the world existed, he *discovered* that it did, or, perhaps one should say, it was *revealed* to him. In truth, the person of Thomas's day did not doubt the world's existence the way a modern idealist or nihilist does, he had never thought of it in the first place. This was a place where he was weak. As a result of his weakness, there was a place that the armor of Christendom had a chink, a big crack. It created a dark nihilism that fed centrally off of the unreality of the world and posited a final monism that denied all; it was a great danger as a hidden enemy to the developing new civilization that would be Europe. Is the world and all that is within it really real? The ancient world was never quite sure of the answer to this, just as the great civilizations of the East still are not. Believing the world's existence is only a late triumph of Christianity. Indeed, it may be the central achievement of the medieval period. When Christianity receded, as in the late nineteenth and twentieth centuries, all the old ancient doubts come creeping back. It is different the second time, though. It was one thing for men of long ago to be dim on the reality of things. It is another to apostatize after you have been given the light. One is a sin of ignorance; the other of presumption. The first is quite excusable; the second carries within it the treachery of Judas.

Up to this point, Christianity had not worked out the implications of creation. It had worked out the Trinity, it had worked out who the person of Christ was. Augustine had thought very deeply about God's sovereignty, and many other things. All of these things implied creation, but it was still in the background and the church had not yet, in a head-on way, taken on creation. That is why monism could creep back and feed on this like a black hole that would swallow light. This was an area that was still dark and shadowy in men's minds.

This is why Chesterton is Thomas' twin.[11] He also was very fat, and in a figure, lived a long time ago, although not literally so. He died in 1936. He tried very hard to apply the achievements of the Middle Ages to the

11. Chesterton was far ahead of his time, or maybe he anticipated much of postmodernity by having so thoroughly and intuitively grasped Thomas' pre-modernity. Chesterton's *Orthodoxy*, and his biography of Thomas, *The Dumb Ox*, are not "Thomistic" (in the nineteenth century rationalistic sense) at all, but are very largely presuppositional volumes. Chesterton was far in advance of the then-burgeoning "Thomistic revival" that very slowly moved through a very thorough and fashionable nineteenth century rationalistic foundationalism to Chesterton's intuitive grasp of the deeper truth.

modern world, and jolt us into remembering what they really were and what they really did as opposed to so many of the mythologies of the "dark ages." Some of us would say he did this with considerable success. Thomas discovered the reality of the world, and Chesterton rediscovered it, and tried to reapply it. In Thomas' day, it had never been thought of, and in Chesterton's a new nihilism wanted to kill it.

New discoveries are always accompanied by great certainty and by great joy. Much time is spent just experimenting with the dimensions of the new discovery—its abilities and potentialities. This is, by the way, what came to be known in the modern world as "science." Joy and exuberance is the mark so often of receiving something that is new. For a period of time, you are simply thrilled, and it takes time to get used to it. One of the implications that joyfully came along with this newness of the world was the ease with which God could be proven. This is why we are wrong in our modern apprehension of the proofs. To us, they are dim and to many if not most, quite unpersuasive. It is because we stand in a different place from medieval man. To him, it was the most persuasive thing in the world, because he suddenly had a world in which to stand to be persuaded from. Beyond that, he saw much more than most moderns do. It is reflected in the brightness of the colors of medieval paintings, and of the exploration of space and perspective in them that one begins to observe. We have forgotten what he saw, and how astonishing it was. Even by the time one gets to the age of Pascal, men are becoming jaded. They no longer even appreciate, let alone stand in awe of, the great gift that came to us through the medieval age. Pascal had to find another way to lead men to God. That way had grown dim.

This leads us to the real reason that Chesterton makes so little of the proofs. It is certainly not because he did not appreciate them. It is because he had re-apprehended the same truth as Thomas, but now sees that one must go at it backwards. Instead of nature being the most obvious proof of God's existence, we must first re-remember that, in the first place, it exists. Secondly, it now must be God who saves his own universe in the minds of men, rather than the world showing God or it will fade away into unreality. Finally, one must deal with modern men in the way petulant children are dealt with. Do you *really* want to lose this thing that you, now in your spoiledness, want to throw away and disclaim? Have the true consequences really sunk into your soul? You will have to be shown what it is that you are about to do.

I recently lived through an earthquake. It was fairly mild as earthquakes go, but still an experience. It is most unnerving to awaken to huge buildings being shaken like children's blocks, and to have the ground under you just turn to rolling jelly. It makes all of those old Bible passages come alive about the earth passing away, and the sky being rolled up like a scroll. To really have the world disappear would be the sum total of all that is terrifying. This is what modern man is toying with, and he needs to be shown.

If we live in a time of apostasy from an old truth, we must deal with it differently than it was dealt with in the first place. Giving premarital counseling to a young, engaged couple is quite different from doing marriage counseling for a broken down relationship that is many years in the making and unmaking, and is near to divorce. Dealing with apostates is different from dealing with children who have never heard the truth. Now we must stand Thomas on his head. What was suddenly so obvious and joyous to him after a lifelong "a-ha" experience with discovering the creation, is different now in dealing with old blasé, debauches who have entirely lost their capacity for awe and amazement.

It has only been of late that people have begun to notice the real effect if Thomas didn't succeed in his proofs. The real objections if he did not succeed are almost never objections to God's existence. Curiously, they are objections to the world's existence. This is hardly ever noticed, though, and the opponents crow too soon when they claim that they have shown that God has not been proved. If he has not been proven, it is because men have forgotten what the world really is, and what an amazing thing it is. What has not been *proven* (but was so immediately luminous to Thomas) is that causality is constant and utterly reliable (which no ancient man, including Aristotle, had any very solid grip on). What has not been *proven* is that there is not such a thing as an infinite string of finite causes that go back and back, forever and ever. Thomas did not have to prove it because this would mean that there is no final explanation, and therefore no ground for any explanations. What has not been *proven* is that the world is not its own explanation *in toto*, which, again, means there are no explanations and, therefore, no proofs. What has not been *proven* is that there is a design in the world everywhere, which would make it possible for arguments to be about something (for arguments cannot demonstrate perfect chaos). The defects are all found in the world, not in God. Thomas had not yet achieved perfect indifference, or that degree of modern sophistication that glories in the absurd. Like a child, he was quite sure of the reality of reliable and constant causality, and of the reality of design everywhere, and of the impossibility of *pure* contingency, or of death like rationalism that made everything to be a final block of ice. His naivety abounded to such an extent that he imagined that reason was *for* something, and that when he thought about something, the coherence and correspondence that seemed to be the consequence were not an accident or a mistake. He actually gloried in these things.

If in fact, the world does exist, then the proofs are meant to tell us all about it. They tell us what the conclusion of the world is, which is God, the God of the Bible. If one was still not quite sure, still not quite convinced, then he could grant the world for arguments sake. Then, further certitude becomes part of the function of the conclusion of the argument. God is certainly the conclusion, but he is also the guarantor of the premises. It works both ways. If there is a God, there is also a world, just as if there is a world, there is then a God.[12]

If the Catherists were right, or the modern nihilists are right, and there is no guarantee of a world in which reason and sensibility can exist, then the very people who overthrow the proofs ought to be brave enough to admit that they are no longer sure of any such thing as reason, or existence, or even of proofs, but they hardly ever do. They will tell you that Thomas has failed, but fail to tell you that Thomas was one of the first people to make possible the dictum of Voltaire: "I may disagree with you, but I will defend to the death your right to disagree." If in some form, Thomas is not right, there is not enough of a world left to even disagree with him. If the final statement of the universe is that "it just is," and that it is self-contained in itself, then there is nothing to say, because you have to be able to put some predicates to the subject, and you no longer have any assurance of being able to do this at all. To disagree with him, you would have to have a stable world of constant and predictable causality, and of discernible design, and of a place in which some point can be made because it all has a final point. Thomas gave you a world in the first place so other disagreements were possible. Side with his enemies, though, and the dark night of real randomness, and sheer non-existence will overcome you. You have shot your weapon of reason and argument and dialectic right out from your own hand.

I had a professor in college who was a lapsed Catholic. One day he commented in an off-handed way, about something that Chesterton had written. He said that it was a very insightful thing to say, but of course it "came from that narrow Catholic framework." I thought to myself then, and

12. This does not imply the necessity of this world, or the necessity of creation. The world is not a corollary to God, and does nothing to complete him. He simply guarantees the existence and rationality of the world in which we do actually live.

I think even more so now, "Narrow, compared to what? Your own modern analytical framework that analyzes and parses words, and is all stuck somewhere inside your own head?" I am not a Catholic, but I share with orthodox Catholics all of the grandness and greatness and hugeness of angels, and archangels, and the infinite triune God who has created heaven and earth. My professor was, of course, confusing these great realities with the narrowness of the Irish Catholic parish of his childhood, no doubt peopled by relatively ignorant, untraveled priests, and even more ignorant and narrow people. Even in their uneducated narrowness, though, through their Catholic faith, they had a window on such vastness as my professor—in his then-current spiritual state—had even lost the capacity to imagine, let alone hope for. It was comic to imagine that what occupied his bald Irish head had much space about it at all.

Thomas gave the most interesting definition of sloth that I have ever seen anywhere, indeed that I can even imagine. He said that sloth was the refusal of joy.[13] Let me suggest that people reject Thomas' discovery and argument, because they are intellectually and spiritually slothful. In his day, it would have meant the refusal of the discovery of creation. In our day, it means the same thing. It is simply too much effort, it is too hard to begin to imagine, too hard to work through the idea that it might be true. If you did, though, truth could be saved, and so could the world. And *that* would be joy. It is a lot to sacrifice for a little ease.

13. Nault, "Acedia," 247.

8

The Kenny Letters

A NUMBER OF YEARS ago, I had interaction with a young missionary who was serving in Central America for an American denomination. He was losing his faith, and what was left of it was in tatters. These are three posts that involved interactions with him. Only my posts are here. I hope they are self-explanatory and comprehensible even though his interactions aren't present.

LETTER I

Dear Kenny,

Thanks for your bio. I enjoyed it immensely. One short note of amusement. When I read over your bio the first time, I thought you said that you "led an inner city *torturing* ministry for three years." With what we northerners know about what is said about South and Central America, it seemed especially good preparation. (He had actually said he was leading an "inner city *tutoring* ministry")

I was fascinated with what you said about evidence, and not even finding that sort of incontrovertible evidence on the mission field, where it is so often purported to be. Surely nothing that would convince your unbelieving father (who may be looking over your shoulder in your mind's eye). But, I think evidence in the Bible is an odd sort of thing. I think everybody at some time wishes to see the "incontrovertible," but the Bible seems to raise interesting questions about that. The three periods in biblical history when there were plethoras of (presumably) that sort of evidence, it didn't do any good. The Children of Israel surely saw enough, one would think, to convince anybody, when they came out of Egypt. But apparently, very few believed. It hardly convinced a soul. And, of course the same is true of both the period of Elijah and Elisha. And finally of course, Jesus own visit to earth. One could set it up like this: "If only God Himself would visit us in visible form, converse with us, and display the very powers of a Creator; then faith would follow." Better yet, "I would believe." But everybody knows what the outcome of just that visit was. He was crucified, and the nation was *hardened* in unbelief. Just an aside: this is an odd literary way to treat these accounts of evidence if one is trying to persuade. All one can say is it is odd, odd, odd.

There is what amounts to a paradigm case in John 12. A voice speaks to Jesus that the text implies is the Father. But the crowd standing by said that it "thundered," or was an "angel." After that, it says that Jesus "hid" from them. And then . . ."Though he had done so many signs before them, yet they did not believe in him."

The point that I am making is that the Bible has its own internal "theology" of doubt and unbelief. And unbelief (it is plain as a pikestaff) is not some "modern" phenomena. In fact, one way to read the Bible is that it is entirely a book devoted to speaking to and exposing unbelief as the "normal" state of man. To be able to believe (the Bible seems clearly to state) is itself a miracle, and to not believe is normal, natural state of our spiritual diseasedness.

Pascal says, somewhere in *The Pensees*, that the true religion would have to be able to account for God's "hiddenness," because it is plain that God IS hidden, or he doesn't exist. (Note above that Jesus "hid" from the people, and it seems a metaphor for God himself making himself unfindable.)

If you will permit me to indulge myself a little, I want to repeat some things that I wrote not too long ago. John 12 carries on with the "theology of unbelief," and it is at least worthwhile seeing what the Bible itself says about the matter.

To explain the unbelief, John goes on to quote Isa 6, which is Isaiah's call. Isaiah's call is a terrible one. He is called to preach, being told ahead of time that all that his ministry will produce is unbelief—in fact, unbelief to the point that God will destroy the nation as punishment. Isa 6:9–10 are a paraphrases of Ps 115:4–7 and Ps 135:15–17. Look them up. Both psalms then go on to say, "Those who make them are like them; so are all who trust in them." (i.e., if you worship a rock, you will become a rock. Seeing you will not see, hearing you will not hear. Rocks don't see or hear, and neither will you if you worship them.)

In the psalms, those ideas are applied to the heathen surrounding Israel, and this is why they do not see or worship Jehovah. But in Isaiah, this terrible reality is applied to Israel. Israel now worship idols, and now cannot see or hear. God is "wholly hidden." Jesus repeatedly quotes this Isaiah passage in the NT, especially in reference to why he teaches in parables (which makes his teaching "hidden"—Matt 13:14–15). Now, an interesting question to ask is, why does the NT quote these passages in reference to the Jews of Jesus time since idolatry is precisely what they were cured of in the Babylonian captivity? And the answer seems to be that there is a new and more damning kind of idolatry now than before. The Pharisees perhaps especially, became (in Bonhoeffer's words) "men of conscience." The law was reified, and human effort was exalted. The Jews, in other words, became their own source of righteousness, and did not submit to the gift of Divine righteousness. Put simply, the Jews no longer worshiped rocks and blocks of wood, they now worshiped themselves. The effect was that God himself could stand right before them, and do mighty works of Creation, and they found it impossible to "see" or "hear" anything.

This is strikingly modern. Since the Enlightenment, Western man has progressively deified himself and his own reason and conscience (finding a kind of apogee in Kant). And through this time, God has become progressively more "silent" and "invisible." In fact, the odd thing is that in this condition, the more one looks, the more one listens, the more there is nothing (and this follows, and is dictated precisely from, the Kantian and post-Kantian epistemology). The most "intelligent" see the least. May I suggest this is precisely the irony that the Bible foretells? And it foretells it as a judgment. Modern western Europeans and (increasingly) Americans are the modern Jews. "They have stumbled over the stumbling stone, as it is written, 'Behold, I am laying in Zion a stone that will make men stumble a rock that will make them fall'" (Rom 9:32b–33). Christ becomes the source of unbelief.

Now, I live in Boulder, Colorado, and people seem to know all about Boulder when I travel around. Boulder is an egghead town and is properly named. It is as hard as a rock, and very few here "see" or "hear." I don't do very much evangelism here. I rarely try to win people to faith. Instead, I try to help people "see" that they are in fact dogmatic unbelievers. They will believe almost anything (New Age theology, "angel guides," astrology, Hinduism, Buddhism, as well as old-fashioned university reductionism, with the University of Colorado being here) before they will believe that Jesus is the Messiah. But there is a great deal of self-deception. People here largely want what is promised with the coming of Messiah. They want Messianic results; they want some facsimile of the New Jerusalem (a little more psycho-therapy, a little more grant money—and it will come). People want it all without the Messiah. I sometimes work hard to encourage people *not* to believe, to be clear and honest about their unbelief. It can make people very uncomfortable. When they have to face it, a great deal of other stuff evaporates, and they are left with nothing. This encourages me, because the promise that Jesus gave is that when the Holy Spirit comes, he will convict people of their sin, "because they do not believe in me" (John 16:9). People sometimes have to stumble very badly over the stumbling stone before there is any hope. Jesus has actually won. He has set the whole agenda. Unbelief in the end defines as much as belief does in the believer. It is a backhanded admission that Jesus *is* the Messiah. After Jesus, there is nowhere to go but nowhere. It is impossible to go back to being a pagan. There is nothing.

If you will permit me a little impudence, you are on the road to nothing. You may still believe something, but if you are a careful scholar going the direction you are going, you will very brilliantly end with nothing, and even see it as a triumph of the intellect. But it is not honest unbelief. It is the unbelief of the reification of the intellect and conscience. It is the unbelief that at the outset already declared that intellect and conscience are autonomous, and therefore *by definition* have no need of God or of Messiah. It is a slight of hand trick. Let me by all means encourage you on your road. Do all you can to prove the text corrupt, mythological, late and unscientific. Carry your reductionisms to the utter end. There is nothing that autonomy cannot explain as autonomy. In the end, you will have no reason to believe in thought or even consciousness (there is nothing there that cannot be explained and explained away by the geneticists, biologists, and sociologists). But in all likelihood, you comfort yourself by wanting all of the things that Messiah came to bring without the supernatural Messiah. But stop kidding yourself. These are all impulses that can easily be explained by the psychologists, and sociologists. They are nothing.

Yours, Rich

LETTER II

Kenny,

Thank you for your response. I'll grant that the last paragraph of my letter was pretty bald and I made some leaps without filling in the gaps. My basic point about the nothingness was this: there is a reductionism that you are applying to the biblical text that has a strong naturalistic aroma about it. That kind of reductionism is a modern mood and an epistemological program. It can be applied to any and everything and it has been. It doesn't just stop with higher criticism, it goes on and on like an acid and eats everything that is human if it is applied consistently. But almost no one has the courage to spill these acids with equal opportunity consistency. This is what is so wonderful about Nietzsche. He did. And he despised as cowards and weaklings people who wouldn't face up to implications. So what we get instead are cadres of people who stop believing in Jesus but go on believing that we ought to feed the hungry, clothe the naked, heal the sick, and generally go about doing good. And, it is very difficult to get people to ask themselves questions about "why?" after they have stopped believing. John Wesley and General Booth loved the poor and cared for them (magnificently) because they loved Jesus, and wanted to do what he commanded. They could tell you quite smartly why they did what they did. The basic questions were not a stumbling stone. But try to get a modern secular liberal, for example, to tell you why he wants to care for the poor. He does it out of habit from generations of chapel-going, and it is in his bones. But it is difficult to keep in the heart, because the heart begins to be empty. Caring for the poor is a reflex and a result of homesickness for the old but lost beliefs that warmed his ancestors. The net result is that usually in the end, cynicism, doubt, and exhaustion are overwhelming, and hands on care seems more and more futile. The truth is that caring for the poor is utterly unromantic, and apart from very strong religious impulse, it simply stops being done, or one hopes that impersonal agencies will do the work. That is what I was driving at about people wanting Messianic results without the Messiah (and how in the end, self-defeating it is).

It is very difficult, in short term, to make the points about reason and consciousness, but briefly, if you carry the naturalistic program out with consistency, the very building blocks of knowledge and existence are knocked out. A naturalistic explanation of reason, consciousness and conscience becomes self-defeating. The program of naturalism is to *see through* what men once thought was explicable by recourse to God, and show that it is rather explicable by the immanent and the material (just like the biblical text). But if reason, consciousness, and conscience can be "explained away" and "seen through," then there is nothing left to explain and nothing left to see. One has at that point "seen through" existence, and existence no longer exists. There is no good reason to stop with your naturalism at the biblical text. The program should be carried through. I want to push you to some deeper level of consistency. Most people want to be reductionist in some area or other, and often feel liberated by seeing through *that*, but then find in the end there is a snake in the bottom of the bottle that bites in places where they wanted to be left comfortably alone. But really, one cannot pick and choose and be fair. If naturalism is "true," it is true for the whole field of reality, and not just patchwork areas. If Jesus is Lord, he is by definition Lord of *all*, and not just of the mountains or the plains. That's what I mean by cheating. You may be liberated from fundamentalism, but did you also count on being liberated from the benefits that legitimately flow from God being the Creator and Redeemer (like being the image of God as a man, and instead being a machine, or at best a highly developed animal)? Did you count on reason being reduced (as a consequence) to atoms crashing into each other in your brain, and therefore thought not being about anything "true," but rather just a secretion (with no truth value at all as a result)?

I assume you are not a missionary for mercenary reasons, but if naturalism is "true" why are you a missionary? You seem to have some ethic you are living out, but if Jesus is not the Lord, why are you trying to do something like what the Sermon on the Mount tells you to do?

Conscience is another phenomena that the naturalistic program can explain away in wholly sociological terms. Apply your program here. Is there anything unique in your ethical sense that a good reductionist psychologist or sociologist cannot explain and explain away wholly in terms of conditioning? I think not. Your conscience is in as bad a shape as you seem to think the church and Christendom are.

You are quite right about modern science being a result of and stepchild of Christianity. Modern science is based on five assumptions, all of them theological.

1. The universe is *rational* reflecting both the intellect and faithfulness of its Creator . . .

2. The universe is *accessible* to us, not a closed book but open to our investigations. Minds created in the image of the mind of God can understand the universe God created.

3. The universe has *contingency* to it, meaning things could have been different from the way we find them . . . (hence) knowledge comes by observing and testing it.

4. There is such a thing as *objective* reality. Because God exists and sees and knows everything, there is truth behind everything. Reality has a hard edge to it and does not cave in or shift like sands in the desert in response to our opinions, perceptions, beliefs, or anything else.

5. There is a *unity* to the universe. There is an explanation—one God, one equation, or one system of logic—which is fundamental to everything. The universe operates by underlying laws, which do not change in an arbitrary fashion from place to place, from minute to minute. There are no loose ends, no real contradictions. At some deep level, everything fits.[1]

Now the oddity is, carry through your program of "scientific reductionism" and you destroy every theological assumption that science is based on. You don't just destroy the biblical text, you destroy the ground you were standing on in the first place. Father Stanley Jaki has wonderfully given his life to just the study of the Christian roots of modern science, and any and all of his books are wonderful. Apart from these theological assumptions, science becomes a modern "habit" rather like modern do goodism, but has no real foundation (because the foundation is all in the doctrine of God, of creation, and of providence). I'll carry on in another letter, this one is getting too long.

Yours, Rich

LETTER III

Kenny,

My point about evidence wasn't that the search for or desire for evidence is not legitimate, but rather that the Bible indicates we are prejudiced and jaundiced in our reception of evidence. We are already predisposed against

1. Ferguson, *Fire*, 8–9.

it, because we have "divinized" ourselves. By "divinized" I meant that we have declared our own reason to be ultimate (rather like the Sadducees), and that reason need not bow the knee and submit to God to function properly. Likewise, like the Pharisees, we have declared our own consciences to be autonomous, and we do not need to receive the law as given, rather we are creators of the law, of morality. From the Enlightenment on, the idea has become very prevalent that if there is any saving to be done, it will be done by ourselves. We work out our own salvation with reason and moral effort. The idea that reason is a participation, in a somewhat pantheistic way, in the Divine, is a very old idea explicitly outlined by Aristotle in his *Metaphysics*. To him, the reasonable part of us *is divine*. Kant (and almost all following thinkers) banished that metaphysical realm, but maintained the absolute ultimacy of reason as something in an uncreated way a thing unto itself, never submitting to any revelation (in fact banishing revelation as even a possibility). Whatever you understood me to mean by making mankind divine, what I meant is along these lines, and it demonstrably happens all the time. It has implications for capacity to receive evidence.

Now there are plenty of empirical evidences, and there are major evidences, especially for the Resurrection (which is very difficult to overthrow). But we are prejudicial in our reception of such evidences because deep down we have already declared our independence from God, and hence refuse to recognize ourselves as either creatures or sinners in need of redemption. The Resurrection does not fit my "grid" or my preconceived notions about myself and the human race, so it makes no difference.

You asked if there was anything in my congregation that could not be naturally accounted for by an unbelieving skeptic. My answer would be emphatically yes, but you will think me cheating when I tell you what they are. My congregation is filled with people who have been washed in the blood of the lamb, who have had their sins forgiven, who have been justified, and sanctified. No naturalist can account for any of these things. They have come to participate in the salvation of God. You will accuse me of begging the question, and of assuming what I need to prove, but my point is that the naturalist begs the question himself. He pretends he is searching for evidence that his epistemological grid has already ahead of time dogmatically declared cannot exist. So even if a man were to rise from the dead there would be a natural explanation for it and it could not mean what, say, the Apostle Paul says it means.

Now, let me move from the theoretical to the practical. Everybody who is a "searcher" needs theoretical help. There are people on this line who can give better help of that sort than me. But there is also the practical and volitional side. The fall seems to have been most centrally located in the will. It was a choice. And hence finding our way back seems also to be a choice, or a series of choices. If it is true that our "receptors" to God have been damaged, there may be choices, and costly ones at that, that we may have to make to once again "see" and "hear."

I can sympathize with your account of spending (I assume) heartbreaking time trying to find a miracle, or a clarity and experience of God in your earlier years, and not finding it. I went through something very similar, and spent a number of years close to despair at the "brass heavens." God was nowhere. For all of my desperation, I could not "find" him. Then I met some people who were able to help me. What they helped me to see was that if we are to find God, and to find a real and living experience of Christ, it will be in the midst of a moral war that I must wage with my-self. The only way that Christ can ever be found is when I am thrown on, most specifically, an utter need for a Savior who can save me from sin. That meant I had to begin to take sin seriously in a way that I never had before. Before (and I was raised in the church), I was caught up in seeking "experiences," and happiness, and (in a youthful way) success (of which I had little of any adolescent sort).

I was encouraged to do a serious moral inventory of my life, and when I did, like C. S. Lewis, I found myself to be a "zoo of lusts." I had flattered myself seriously, and had never known myself. The level of dishonesty, impurity, and sloth that I found was appalling. The truth is that like Orual of C. S. Lewis' *Til We Have Faces*, I was forced to "remember" my life for the second time very differently than I had habitually always viewed it (I, the idealist, the victim, who found self-pity somehow profound). I was given clarity one day when I sat down to concretely face myself in the light of Christ's standards that seemed a "miracle." God seemed quite willing to help me see sin, a question I had never before bothered to ask him help with.

To avoid vagueness, my friends encouraged me to write it down—everything—as far back as I could remember in detail. Curiously, it freed me from vague self-loathing (which I was filled with, and had always mistaken for some kind of Christian virtue) and gave me a sense of both peace and orientation. But then, they were even harder on me. They told me I needed to find someone I trusted and confess every detail of my life to him.

I shrank from this. It would forever destroy my cherished self-image if I told these things. But, they said, I needed to do it not so much to unburden myself, as to maximize my sense of sin. "A small sense of sin means a small sense of Christ," they used to say. There were three things that I was so ashamed of—I thought I could never tell anyone. But I did, and for the first time, moral transparency began to enter my life (a very lonely one) and the reality of real friendship began to open up (more people are lonely than will ever admit it).

But then they were even harder on me. I should go and do restitution for things I had stolen, and I should make amends to people I had wronged. I began to do that. It was unbearably hard, and truly humbling.

What I began to find was that in every way, I was up against it. I had no moral power to change the "zoo of lusts" that I found in myself. And my guilt was overwhelming. I began to break down and had a sense of my lost-ness, and went through very dark weeks. My sense of moral self-sufficiency just collapsed. Then, the most marvelous thing happened. Christ came, and he came as exactly what he promised he was—a Savior from sin. I "experienced" forgiveness. It was quite luminous. I began to "hear" him, and know an inner teaching that I had always hoped was real, but could never find. The platitudinous phrase of evangelicalism became real—I began to have "a personal relationship" with Christ, and it was unmistakable.

Just today, I met with someone who is in real trouble in his life. He has been raised in the church, but it has never "taken." I asked him what his major sin was. He said immediately that it was hatred and resentment. Everything else hung on that for him (we are all "depravity specific." We have differences that are quite individual). I told him to make a list of all the people he has hurt, and been resentful toward, and go make amends to as many as he can. He said that he wasn't sure there was enough time left in his life to do it—but he is going to, I believe. He has never faced this simple reality, ever—and he has been around the church and Christian schools all his life.

Certitude and assurance come through facing sin. The only evidence that will ever do you any final good is that he can save you from who you are as a sinner. That is what he has promised, and that is where you must look for him. Everywhere else, he is hidden.

Yours, Rich

9

The Uniformity of Nature and Biblical Authority

> So oddly, biblical miracles (as opposed to pagan magic) and science are twin brothers with the same patrimony, and they came from the same household. Originally they were not enemies or rivals of one another, but actually implied each other.[1]

THE BIBLE AND NATURE

I RECENTLY LISTENED (ON an electronic reader) to three lectures by the great philosopher of science, Michael Polanyi. A point struck me quite forcefully that was *not* a point he had set out to make, but was most interesting and compelling.

Polanyi was discussing the necessary hallmark of tradition and remaining within the tradition (showing that science itself is as dependent upon a tradition just as much as, say, Talmudic studies). He was pointing out what experimental evidence ought to be accepted and what ought not be accepted. It is simply not the case that all experimental evidence is found to be acceptable. A good deal of it is too far outside of the parameters of the "tradition" and is, therefore, simply ignored, or "put on hold" or re-interpreted, or regarded as being the result of faulty experimental technique and therefore, simply mistaken. Sometimes, data that is apparently contradictory leads to a new, larger way of interpreting data that brings reconciliation from larger

---

1. Bledsoe, "A Visit To Orthodoxy."

parameters. However, it is impossible to accept all experimental data at face value. If all the data were accepted, science would end.[2]

Some of the data (and he gives fascinating examples) demonstrate startling things, and if simply believed and taken into the corpus, would lead us to no longer believe in the uniformity of nature, or that it is possible to give a rational account of how the universe functions. Face acceptance would lead us back to a pagan belief that magic and irrationality are supreme. It would lead us to believe that, in fact, as Ovid believed and wrote about in his *Metamorphosis:* anything can turn into anything else.

These conclusions are banished from the outset, though, because the uniformity of nature and the rationally penetrable universe are axioms that are believed *a-priori*. Whatever violates those axioms are automatically thrown out. Nature's uniformity and universal rationality are not provable dogmas, but are assumptions that all of science depends upon.

Where did these axioms come from?

Polanyi is himself Hungarian, and to understand where these axioms came from, one can turn to one of the other great Hungarian minds of the twentieth century: Stanley Jaki.[3] Jaki demonstrates that science is the stepchild of the Christian church and the Hebrew and Christian scriptures.

Here is a short synopsis of what I had learned initially from Cornelius Van Til, the great Reformed thinker, but secondarily from the great Jaki:

> Greek metaphysics by themselves, could not support the modern scientific enterprise. The Greeks did not believe in the pervasive rationality of the universe. Ultimately form could not encapsulate matter, and there was always an excrescence of the irrational. Modernity would never have happened had it not been for Christianity and the church in the western world. The ancient world was ruled by various forms of pantheism (the idea that the cosmos itself is in some sense divine) and the many gods that emerged out

2. "The process of explaining away deviations is in fact quite indispensable to the daily routine of research. In my laboratory I find the laws of nature formally contradicted at every hour, but I explain this away by the assumption of experimental error. I know that this may cause me one day to explain away a fundamentally new phenomenon and to miss a great discovery. Such things have often happened in the history of science, Yet I shall continue to explain away my odd results, for if every anomaly observed in my laboratory were taken at its face value, research would instantly degenerate into a wild-goose chase after imaginary fundamental novelties." Polanyi, *Science, Faith, and Society*, 12.

3. The three great Hungarian thinkers of the twentieth century were Polanyi, Jaki, and Arthur Koestler. All three knew and influenced each other, and all three dealt extensively with the philosophy and history of science.

of the forms and chaos of the cosmos. It was a world of polytheism, and a world in which anything could, in some mysterious sense, become a concentration point for the demonic powers that the world was filled with. For example, rocks, trees, animals, men, could rise up and become divine powers themselves. Then, Christianity declared that the world and the cosmos were the creation of the one triune God who was exhaustively in control of all that there was, even in spite of the fall into sin and the consequent rebellion that now characterized all things. Christ, through whom all things were created, came to redeem all things from the rebellion that now marked us, and his church was the center point of his presence and of his work in the world in the new era inaugurated by his death, resurrection, and ascension into heaven where he sat down at the right hand of the Father. One of the names of Christ is "the logos," which has many shades of meaning, which include both word or speech, and logic (*logos* is the root of our English word logic). If the world was created through the one who was both the reality of language and logic, it meant that the cosmos itself was reasonable, and could be spoken of. It was not ineffable. In other words, the world could be studied and understood. This great theological reality was what swept away the old pagan cosmos that was irrational, unpredictable, and controlled by demonic and magical powers. The one, true God was a God of both reason and speech, and his creation mirrored that. Hence, while the existence of God is what makes miracles possible, it is also the foundation of what came to be termed the uniformity of nature, which means that the world is a place of constant causality and stable and rational construction. The Christian doctrines of the Trinity and of creation were, in fact, the foundation of modern science. Oddly, biblical miracles (as opposed to pagan magic) and science are twin brothers with the same patrimony, and they came from the same household. Originally they were not enemies or rivals of one another, but actually implied each other.[4]

Just as the world is the "book" of the scientist, so the Bible is the "world" of the Christian. The uniformity of nature, and the rationality of cosmos are axioms (ultimately derived from the Bible) that cannot be ultimately empirically established, or contradicted. Rather, they are assumptions that make science possible in the first place. Likewise, inerrancy and infallibility are axioms that are also derived from the Bible[5] and it is also the case

4. Bledsoe, "Visit to Orthodoxy."
5. Warfield, *Inspiration and Authority.*

that inerrancy can be neither empirically demonstrated nor contradicted. It is an axiom, a doctrine that makes the very doing of theology possible in the first place.[6]

Scientific progress is almost always a result of dealing with "evidence" that appears to undo science, evidence that if taken at face value, would in fact undo the rationality of the universe, or the uniformity of nature. Science, in other words, progresses as a result of finding a coherent and consistent explanation of a "problem."

Likewise, theology is only possible if revelation is a coherent and consistent whole (i.e., the inerrancy and infallibility of the whole of the Bible is the basis of knowing what we know about God and his dealing with his world). Problems, or elements or facts that appear to contradict the coherence and consistency of the Bible are, if taken in the proper spirit, the very foundation of progress and the forward movement of theology and of our knowledge of God and his action in his world. Oddly, theologians over the last two hundred years, often in the name of science, have surrendered the integrity of the Bible because of "problems." In fact, especially with "higher textual critics," the default position is almost always to claim a contradiction. Multiple editors, conflation of texts and anachronistic "reading back into" earlier texts by later editors are almost automatically assumed at the first hint of any apparent difficulty. This is the practice, even when the results are obviously silly and very easy and less contorted explanations are immediately obvious. There is almost a compulsive addiction to declaring contradiction.

This is the end of theology, just as a similar loss of courage in the face of strange and difficult data for the scientist would be the end of science. The scientists would immediately release us back to a world of myth, superstition, and magic; the theologians have certainly done so.

---

6. What one observes in both science and theology is a non-vicious circle of demonstration. In science, uniformity of nature and the rationality of the cosmos, and in theology, inerrancy and infallibility are not empirically demonstrable. However, "subordinate" demonstration is possible. With every fresh triumph of science in giving a new rational explanation to what appears to be contradictory, greater confidence is gained in believing the a-priori axioms. The same is true with the Bible. The more one finds the Bible giving coherent explanation to what previously had appeared an irrational world, or as deeper coherence is demonstrated in what previously appeared odd and contradictory, the more ones confidence in the truth of the doctrines of inerrancy and infallibility is strengthened. Some reconciliations are so wonderful and remarkable that they constitute veritable "ah-ha" moments. They are the very foundation of "fun." Fun is given up when one surrenders and loses ones courage. One is then thrown back to myth, superstition and magic.

"Fun" is a strange reality and perhaps difficult to define. Whatever it is, it is wonderful. The "fun" of science is when a "contradiction" is given larger and better coherent explanation. For example, this is the outcome when that which contradicts Newtonian mechanics and the results of Michelson-Morley experiments leads to the theory of relativity.[7] The sense of crystalline beauty, aesthetic pleasure felt in the coherence of relativity has been expressed by many as the theory gave a new and deeper coherence to what appeared previously to be a tatters. At the very least, Einstein's insight was immense fun.

Theologians have often been killjoys. They need to learn something new about fun, and have the courage to experience it.

FUN, CREATIVITY, AND THEOLOGY AND SCIENCE

My interest here is less apologetic—in the sense of trying to make the Bible and its doctrines somehow palatable to modern rationality—and is more along the lines of giving a check on our unbounded, and stifling egotism, which also destroys all creativity.

The scientist is able to be truly "creative" in large measure because he is disciplined by the cosmos that is really "out there." He might have all kinds of opinions that he would like to be true, that he would even like to impose on the world and the cosmos. If he were a magician, he could do exactly that. He could say the magic words, and the cosmos would obey him and do his bidding. However, "reality" is intransigent, and will not just bend to our wishes. Reality, since it is the creation of the real and living God, is also far more interesting than anything we could make up. Therefore, reality opposes my petty little wishes with real experimental data that opposes my petty little wishes. It is frustrating at first, but if I allow myself to be disciplined, the end discovery is far more interesting than my small and petty imagination could have possibly invented. Newtonian mechanics appear to be violated again and again with Michelson-Morley, so I become increasingly sure that I am not dealing with flawed data, and the final outcome in a great new coherence is the general theory of relativity. Relativity

---

7. The Michelson Morley experiments demonstrated that the speed of light was constant in every direction from a moving platform (and one can picture the earth itself as a moving platform). The forward speed of the platform did not make the light travel faster, whether the light moved forward with the platform, or slower if it went backward in the opposite direction. Newtonian physics could not account for this.

is far more interesting than what my petty, magic desiring imagination could have conceived of in the first place. I have been disciplined by reality.

The same happens when I use the Bible as my infallible guide. I am naturally as a fallen creature, overwhelmingly egotistical, and I want to be a magician who "invents" all realities. In fact, what my fallen and petty imagination constantly "invents" is boring, oppressive, stupid, and "uncreative." I believe I will create a utopia. Instead, I create a "dystopia" like Orwell saw in *1984* or like Huxley foresaw in *Brave New World*. The real Kingdom of God disciplines me. Apart from a text that I am subject to, I just constantly cave in on myself, and I am back to my own oppressive boredom.

I'd like to provide some examples of this, both big and small:

First, a *big* example: The New Testament offers us a mass of strange and seemingly contradictory texts about the nature of God. The real adventurers are the ones who submit themselves to the text and find the really big coherence (Athanasius, Augustine). Nicene Orthodoxy, by the fourth or fifth century, has hammered out the doctrines of the Trinity and Incarnation. Really big, really interesting ideas—like relativity. When I make myself the source and the maker of all coherence and all boundaries, then I am left with all of the unresolved dilemmas of the paganism that has gone before. I can do no better than Arianism, Tri-Theism, and Modalism.[8]

Here is a *small* example: In Deut 21:18–21, the law of the rebellious son, the modern progressive or liberal looks at it and says: "See what a barbaric book the Bible is? How wonderful that we now have the freedom and liberty to say that this ancient book—which in our own way, we of course revere—is *wrong* and *mistaken*. Yes, it is filled with culture-bound patriarchal privilege, along with some interesting mythologies, and some helpful things. But the Old Testament is in favor of killing your own children. How evil. How terrible. How wonderful that we have arrived and are now superior to so much that went before us. How wonderful that we have risen above our forbearers and have arrived!"

What if there is a deeper coherence that is far more interesting than declaring our own superior progressive insight?

This passage is, in fact, to my knowledge the first and only place in the ancient world that contradicts the doctrine of *pater familias*, the doctrine that the father "owns" his family and can carry out discipline all the way up

---

8. Arianism said Jesus was only a god; Tri-Theism said that Father, Son, and Spirit were three distinct gods, and Modalism said Father, Son, and Spirit were just three different and separate hats that one god put on at different times.

to putting his family members to death with no legal consequence[9]. In this law, the rebellious son is taken outside the family to the elders. Clan and family power is limited. This is to be done by the father *and the mother*, and this is absolutely unique as well. She is as empowered as the father to take him to state courts. Finally, there is not a single known instance of a son being so put to death in all of Jewish history, except, oddly and interestingly, in the case of Jesus. The charge against him was that he was "a glutton and a wine bibber" and he *was* put to death as a rebellious son (Matt 11:19). This is radically different from ancient law all the way up through Roman law, which upheld *pater familias*.

Here is the other irony, which I see happening again and again. The liberal, who assumes their moral superiority by claiming the superior moral insight of their own autonomous moral conscience (which heroically defies the Bible and declares its own superior insight) are themselves wholly dependent on what the Bible created in the first place. We live in a world where parents and fathers do not kill their own offspring. This did not pop into place the moment we declared our own Cartesian independence, but was created by the Old Testament law.

Hence, so often what strikes us as odd, strange, incoherent, in the text of the Bible, is really, when more deeply understood, the very foundation of wonderful, new insight.

9. I owe this to Dennis Prager.

10

Origins and Truth

THE SELF-CONTRADICTION OF NATURALISM

Much of this little volume hangs on the reality of Adam and Eve in the Garden of Eden being real people with a real history in a real place. That is easily dismissed in the current climate. After all, "evolution has proven . . ." and one can finish the sentence. But wait a moment, and let's at least consider a new way.

Here is the conundrum: if straightforward materialistic Darwinism is "true," (Darwinism with no Divine beginning or direction) then Darwinism can't possibly be true. C. S. Lewis writes, "If my mental processes are determined wholly by the motions of atoms in my brain, I have no reason to suppose that my beliefs are true . . . and, hence, I have no reason for supposing my brain to be composed of atoms"[1]—or, for that matter, supposing that the materialistic evolutionary account given of our origins is true either.

Once Christianity comes, the ancient mythologies are banished. Once Christianity is rejected, one returns to myths with the inconvenience that now they are no more believed, or believable to the rejecters, than the Christianity that originally displaced the mythology. What we are left with are ideologies and paradigms that are recognized as no more than organizing structures, but make no claim to being true. The terrible reality for the modern world is that folks who run mental hospitals, prisons, and totalitarian regimes dare to consistently act on "modern truths" (an oxymoron if ever there was one).[2] Everyone else either benignly believes

1. Lewis, *Miracles*, 22; Professor J.B.S. Haldane, *Possible Worlds*, 209.

2. One must hasten to add that it may not just be the inmates in the mental hospitals and prisons who are crazy and criminal, but the keepers quite possibly as well. Foucault's insistence that the modern world (even in what used to be called the "free world") is

nothing (sparing themselves the severities of real consistency that issues in nothing), or still believes in Christianity, or as much vestige of it as their cultural heritage allows them to leave unexamined.

Once Christianity comes and is then rejected, you cannot go back to mythology.[3] But unfortunately, you cannot have "truth" either (you have "seen through" everything). You are stuck. C. S. Lewis' little chapter in his book, *Miracles*, titled "The Self-Contradiction of the Naturalist"[4] reduces straightforward Darwinists and materialists to confusion. Alvin Plantinga has baffled whole rooms full of Darwinists when he has applied the same paradoxes. It's a hard place to be—just where can one place scientific theory if one has the quandary of there not being "truth"?

When Plantinga put forward his elegant refutation of why Darwinism cannot be "true"[5] (an expansion of Lewis' argument), one editor from Naturalism.org, comforted himself by saying, "Not knowing the mind of God (no one does after all) Plantinga can't offer much detail about God's (and our) supernatural truth tracking ability."[6] But the burden of this volume is indeed that we can "know the mind of God."

Unless one simply succumbs to being crazy, incompetent, or criminal, one *has to* assert that one *can* know truth. Apart from God speaking to us, one asserts it out of the blue, believing in reason, truth, goodness, and beauty for no reason at all, or at best, extremely weak reasons, reasons that themselves are built on shantytown, stick foundations that are stuck in a swamp. Contrary to the assertions with no foundation, we assert quite

---

increasingly taking on the characteristics and imitation of the prison, and a writer like Thomas Szasz, who wrote a very influential book calling one of the major tenants of the modern world a complete myth (*The Myth of Mental Illness*) one begins to be left with the assumption that the very tenants of late modernity, as well as its unintended consequences are crazy and criminal.

3. Berkof, *Christ and the Powers*, 47–55.

4. I am not sure anybody has ever said it better than Lewis in his original chapter. It is succinct, clever, devastating, and clear as glass. Unfortunately, he updated the chapter to satisfy the somewhat rarified objections of Elizabeth Anscombe (clarifying the distinction between the "ground" and "cause" of a conclusion) He satisfied Anscombe, and re-writing the chapter may have been an act of almost unparalleled humility (a trait not common in scholars), but it left the chapter also almost incomprehensible to the layman. Anscombe found clarity at one refined point, and the popular public he wrote for no longer had any idea what he was talking about. Lewisian clarity was sacrificed to satisfy one professional philosopher who was already a Christian and really in no need of being persuaded! Lewis, *Miracles*, chapter 3; Hooper, "Truth about Anscombe."

5. Plantinga, *Where the Conflict*.

6. TWC, "Is Naturalism Self-Defeating?"

confidently that indeed we do know something about "the mind of God."[7] God has spoken. One is left with a modern paradox: just what is the mythology here? Are Adam and Eve, and the Garden of Eden mythologies? Slow down. One should not be too quick to judge. Let's try some things on for size and see just how they feel. This book is a kind of dressing room where just that sort of trying on can happen.

THE DRESSING ROOM

We are flying through the sky at five hundred miles per hour when it first occurs to us that we should take note of something; we first get curious about things (back to the second half of chapter 5). We are searching for meaning.

The Bible speaks into this need for meaning in the first two chapters of the first book of the Bible: Genesis. The creation account is one of six creative words. These are fiat words. There is no process in what God speaks. God speaks, and it is so. However, with each fiat word (or sentence) God initiates process. Now, these two things go together: word and process. Fiat word precedes process, and process itself has imbedded within it word. Word is always prior and ultimate.

The ancient world and the late modern world want to content themselves with pure process. If process were all we had, we would never even know there was a process. Process is pure flow, pure Hericlitian flux without word. Real process is orderly and comprehensible. This is why literature, science, philosophy, can meditate upon and understand process. There is a formula, an equation behind all process. A word was spoken into it, and can therefore be read out of it again.

The ancients believed in ages, eons and ages, one piled upon another. Moses, who may have compiled the creation account, was not taught in the midst of Egyptian higher education that the world was of recent origin. The idea of millions and billions of years and even billions of ages is an ancient and pagan idea. It has only returned with modern Darwinian outlook.[8] However, it is precisely this ages and ages outlook, the eons upon eons, that eventually tempts much of paganism to finally retreat to a blank and

---

7. "Now we have received, not the spirit of the world, but the Spirit who is from God, that we might know the things that have been freely given to us by God . . . 'For who has known the mind of the Lord that he may instruct him?' But we have the mind of Christ" (1 Cor 2:12, 16).

8. Jaki, *Science and Creation*.

empty monism as an escape, or as an anodyne to the flux of endless and meaningless time. The speech of God is the basis of all meaning, of all rationality, of all ability to speak of and about the world at all. Were it not for the six-fold word, the world would indeed be a "blooming, buzzing confusion."

Perhaps the primary barrier to believing the Genesis account today is its apparent assertion of a relatively recent beginning point. If one accepts a 24-hour day as the meaning of "morning and evening" and "day," it is difficult to extend the age of the earth (and indeed the universe) to more than a handful of thousand years. Empirical evidence seems to indicate an age of not just millions, but even billions of years. But, if we do not have a "word beginning," one cannot account for meaning and rationality. This is an enormous dilemma, and one not to be minimized.

Here is a simple reconciliation. It is not the only one, but it is the simplest, and at least deserves a hearing. A beginning, by means of a word from the God of speech, works backward as well as forward. When God initiates, he initiates time forward, but processes are also initiated backward. In other words, the world is begun with process being already in the midst of process, not necessarily at the beginning of process.

There is an old and clichéd question: which came first, the chicken or the egg? The answer, according to Genesis, is definitely that the chicken came first. God did not initially just create acorns, but oak trees that are fully grown and mature. Those mature oaks may have had acorns upon them, but they are there as a part of the mature and full plant itself. One argument, for example, in defense of the vast age of the universe, is the fact that light is now reaching us from galaxies that are hundreds of millions of light years away from us. If God created with process already processing, then he conceivably created the world and the surrounding universe with the connecting light beam created as well, and already connected. If one reads from the processes, one will of necessity read age far behind the beginning. An absolute beginning does not entail only forward processes, but processes already initiated, working backward as well.

This would also explain, at least partly, why what is now termed "foundationalism" does not "work." Foundationalism implies that there is some absolute starting point to theoretical knowledge. Even if that is true, what was initiated at the beginning was a fully functioning world that worked backwards as well as forwards. When Adam and Eve were created, they were placed into a world that was already a fully functioning and coherent world with a built in past. Just as we find ourselves already in the midst of a coherent and functioning world, we do not discover it or "justify" our knowledge of it by beginning with some indubitable single starting point, but we know it already as a coherent whole (albeit, not all of it, but already coherent and functioning).

It is also possible to deal with "day" (*yom* in the Hebrew) as an analogical day, and thus able to encompass even millions or billions of years, and still retain the integrity of the Genesis text. The important thing is to offer alternate possible reconciliations of the time issue, and still retain the reality of a literal Adam and Eve and a Garden of Eden.[9]

In any case, in either reconciliation of the text to empirical evidence, it is necessary to retain the priority of creation by word and through word. It is God's creation by means of speech that makes science possible. Pure process would leave all of empirical reality ineffable, incomprehensible, and unknowable.

9. Dr. Vern Poythress, in his very fine book, *Redeeming Science,* offers this as another alternate possible reconciliations of the time issue, and still retains the reality of a literal Adam and Eve and Garden of Eden. I would also recommend any book by Hugh Ross, who writes from a similar perspective. Poythress, *Redeeming Science,* 131–47.

11

Who Is This Man?

IF YOU ARE NOT a believer, Jesus constitutes one of the greatest of stumbling blocks. People loathe being pushed into corners, and resist it with all of their might, but I must press you with the most urgent of all questions: Just what do you do with Jesus? My friend, this is *the* most pressing concern. It is a tremendous problem, and one that is largely "solved" by people by ignoring it. Theologian John Gerstner made one of the most telling statements I have seen on the subjective authority that Jesus exercises even over those who give no allegiance to him. This is the first step in recognizing that there is a mighty problem here.

> The virgin reaction and all the subsequent reactions of the world to Jesus Christ is, then, that he is the ideal, the perfect man, the moral paragon of the race. I do not wish to gloss over the fact that not absolutely everyone has agreed with this verdict. I know that George Bernard Shaw spoke of a time in Christ's life when, as he said, Christ was not a Christian. I know that some have thought that Socrates died more nobly than Jesus: that others believe him to have been morally surpassed. But the overwhelming testimony of the world is to the perfection, the incomparable perfection, of Jesus of Nazareth. The few exceptions could easily be shown to rest on fundamental misconceptions of certain things, which Jesus said or did; and furthermore, the vast majority of those who do take exception usually think that some imagined fault is a failure of Christ to be, as George Bernard Shaw said, a Christian! *They seem to know of no higher standard by which to test Christ that the standard of Christ Himself.*[1]

1. I add the italics of the last sentence for emphasis. In this sentence, Gerstner ironically comes close to being a presuppositionalist. Sproul, *If There Is a God*, 93–4.

Try to paint a persuasive picture of a good man, let alone a perfect one. The problem seems not just beyond ordinary mortals, but beyond the most gifted of the great geniuses as well. Dostoyevsky nearly broke himself on the problem. This was his point in writing *The Idiot*, and in his genius, he gave us Prince Mishkin. Father Zosima in *The Brothers Karamazov* is a further attempt. These are his best and most noble efforts. Yet, he did not quite succeed. He still falls short. Mishkin has a touch of the pathetic and the unstable about him; the great sinner, Ivan, is a fuller character than the Father Zosimov in *The Brothers Karamazov*. True saintliness is the hardest of all real qualities to capture. Painting villains takes real artistry, and artistry is consummated here. But it is broken on goodness. Compare Dante's *Inferno* and *Purgatorio* with the *Paradiso*. Heaven is icy and unreal, but hell and purgatory are quite perfect and persuasive. The romantic critics have all made the fundamental mistake of assuming that because Satan is the most interesting and fullest character in *Paradise Lost*, this is therefore where Milton's real sympathies lay. This is silly. Satan is the most persuasive because Milton, like all of us, was more experimentally acquainted with wickedness than with perfect holiness.[2] Indeed, nobody is experimentally acquainted with perfect holiness. In the human race, outside of Christ (where we have an "invasion" from Heaven by way of incarnation), the last man and woman to be on speaking terms with sinlessness were Adam and Eve. Here one is given the impression that they remained so for at least a good twenty minutes before succumbing to temptation. In every elementary course ever given on "creative writing," the first counsel of the professor is to "write about what you know." Who knows much more than the theory, and only the most elementary practice of goodness? When it comes to sin, all of us have some specialty or other.

There is no fully persuasive picture of goodness in the world except for the gospels. All the pictures that come close to portraying goodness are attempts at Christlikeness. Even when people describe the highest of the sages from entirely different cultures, my experience is that they describe them as Christlike; conversely, I have never heard Christ described as "Buddha-like," or "Socrates-like." Jesus seems to be the incomparable picture everywhere.

Try sometime to decipher Jesus' temperament. He is none and all. He seems to have the fullness of humanity. Yet, he is the most particular of men and not an abstract absolute or abstract ideal in the least. C. S. Lewis

---

2. Lewis, *Preface to Paradise Lost*, 100–1.

noted that only three men in history have the quality of being real people who sometimes meet us as fictional characters in the realistic novel: Plato's Socrates, Boswell's Johnson, and Jesus of the gospels.[3]

In one of Lewis' best formulations, he asks:

> What do you make of him? I am trying here to prevent anyone saying the really foolish thing that people often say about him: "I'm ready to accept Jesus as a great moral teacher, but I don't accept his claim to be God." That is the one thing we must not say. A man who was merely a man and said the sort of things Jesus said would not be a great moral teacher. He would either be a lunatic-on a level with the man who says he is a poached egg-or else he would be the Devil of Hell. You must make your choice. Either this man was, and is, the Son of God: or else a madman or something worse. You can shut him up for a fool, you can spit at him and kill him as a demon; or you can fall at his feet and call him Lord and God. But let us not come with any patronizing nonsense about his being a great human teacher. He has not left that open to us. He did not intend to.[4]

You only have three choices. Oddly, the sense of most people will not permit it to be said that Jesus is either of the first two. The truth presses in very, very hard.

Warfield writes that this way of stating the dilemma goes back to the church father Tertullian, but actually it goes back even further to the gospels themselves.[5] "But who do you say I am?" Jesus asks his disciples. You, too, will have to make a confession about him; he requires it. Jesus virtually forces a confession from men. The horn of the dilemma is posed by Jesus in this terrifying way: Either he does what he does because he is the son of man who has inaugurated the Kingdom of God on earth, or he is a devil. Do you dare, do you really dare to say he is a devil? He warns you to be careful. If one really makes that judgment, then he will commit a blasphemy that Jesus warns is beyond forgiveness. Do you see how he presses you? Even as he warns you, you are being forced to take a stance. Who does he think he is that he can threaten me in this fashion? Yes, that is just the question, and in even formulating your response you may already be veering toward blasphemy. He presses you, and you cannot escape. If he would leave you

3. Lewis, "Modern Theology," 352.
4. Lewis, *Mere Christianity*, 55–56.
5. Warfield, "Misconception of Jesus," 196–237.

alone, then you might ignore it but he presses you. You must chose, and your choice is larger than heaven and earth put together.

In the last two centuries, many theological critics have taken Jesus' family's stance in the assumption that he was unbalanced and needed care.[6] Poor Jesus. He must be protected from himself. Jesus (and by extension, the apostles) had not had the advantages of a good German theological education, so of course he made (and the apostles after), all kinds of elementary mistakes about him. Just as if to rebuke the world in its own idiocy as the learned decided that Jesus was only an unbalanced, or ecstatic visionary, men came along and took just those oddest and hardest sayings of Jesus quite seriously, even literally, and changed the world. This is true of Gandhi, Martin Luther King, and George Müller. Müller was a Christian in the most orthodox way, and his story gives complete demonstration to Jesus' saying, "For your heavenly Father knows that you need all these things. But seek first the kingdom of God and his righteousness, and all these things shall be added to you. Therefore do not worry about tomorrow, for tomorrow will worry about its own things. Sufficient for the day is its own troubles" (Matt 6:32b–34). For fifty years, Müller provided for upwards of ten thousand orphans in his exquisitely run orphanages by never asking anyone, except God in prayer, for a dime (or a pence). His needs and the orphans' needs were all provided.[7] With Gandhi, I am not suggesting that he was a Christian in any orthodox sense, and very likely, Martin Luther King was not either.[8] What I do suggest is that they took some of Jesus' most visionary words with almost complete literalness. They demonstrated that even in the world of "Realpolitik," they obeyed his counsel and imitated his person to the utter surprise of the cynical in the West. Gandhi pricked what existed of the British conscience as it had been formed under the tutelage of Christianity, and called them to their own highest ethical knowledge. He

---

6. To read more about Jesus' family stance, see Matt 12:46–50.

7. I know of no figure who is more encouraging in the modern, cynical, materialistic world than Müller. He was a Prussian who immigrated to England. The son of an administrator, he kept meticulous records for his entire adult life, and meant his life as a demonstration of the reality that God answers prayer. Steer, *Delighted in God*.

8. Methodist missionary E. Stanley Jones gives the best evaluation that I have ever seen of Gandhi. His lament is that Gandhi narrowed himself to an Indian parochial figure when he could have been a world figure. He only imitated Jesus, instead of knowing Jesus as the Lord of heaven and earth. There is a contradiction in choosing the "way of peace" in imitating Jesus, while embracing the *Bhagawad Gita* as your highest religious authority, which begins by glorifying senseless warfare as an inevitable and unalterable fate. Jones, *Mahatma Gandhi*; Jones, *Along the Indian Road*, 127–55.

was an insoluble problem to them. Even though England found the British Empire to be an increasing drain, they left India not because they had to in any military or final economic sense, but because they were ashamed. The same is true of Martin Luther King, whose achievement in America is indubitable at this point, no matter what corruptions may have followed along after him in further race relation developments.

Some say that Gandhi's tactics would never have worked if the masters of India had been, the very non-Christian Soviets, instead of the British.[9] Since the collapse of the Soviet Union, though, one cannot say even this with quite such assurance. That empire itself ended very largely through a movement, which began in Poland, and expanded to "passive resistance," fueled by Pope John Paul II and a large portion of the Catholic population involved in the labor union movement. Poland was the first domino in the row that knocked down all the rest. One sees, in a different instance, that the Chinese communists have never quite gotten away with slaughtering the students who tried Gandhi's tactics in Tiananmen Square.[10] One is amazed that groups like Amnesty International are able so easily to rile and distress petty thugs in third world countries with simple letters appealing to conscience. I do not think that letters pointing out injustice to Genghis Khan in the twelfth century would have bothered him even slightly, even if he had been literate! These days, thugs want their deeds hidden and in the dark; they are at least embarrassed to be seen for what they are. On a very large scale, the effect of moral exposure on the Soviet Union with the publication of *The Gulag Archipelago*, by Solzhenitsyn was devastating. Solzhenitsyn rightly said of himself that the Soviets feared a great writer more than all the armies of the world. His moral authority, which was explicitly

9. Orwell, "Reflections on Gandhi." Orwell wrote, "It is difficult to see how Gandhi's methods could be applied in a country where opponents of the regime disappear in the middle of the night and are never heard of again. Without a free press and the right of assembly, it is impossible not merely to appeal to outside opinion, but to bring a mass movement into being, or even to make your intentions known to your adversary. Is there a Gandhi in Russia at the moment? And if there is, what is he accomplishing? The Russian masses could only practice civil disobedience if the same idea happened to occur to all of them simultaneously, and even then, to judge by the history of the Ukraine famine, it would make no difference."

10. I am not here commending pacifism, but acknowledging that even *in these extreme circumstances*, attempts to imitate Jesus had enormous consequences. It is doubtful that the resistance of the Polish labor movement could, or would have had such huge implications for the final collapse of the U.S.S.R. if in the background, the enormous military and economic might of the United States had not been at hand.

and believingly derived from Jesus Christ, constituted an insoluble crisis for the Soviets. They could not kill him, or silence him without condemning themselves, and they finally stumbled over the rock that he placed in their way. It was reported that later that Gorbachev was very disturbed by Ronald Reagan's reference to the Soviet Union as "an evil empire." It seemed a particular sting to the conscience.[11] The only final explanation I know of for such troubled consciences on the part of some pretty terrible people is that the authority of Jesus Christ had extended, at least a little, into that place by the late twentieth century. It is a side effect of the missionary movement and of the church.

I remember a number of years ago hearing John Lennon claim, with boyish and stupid brashness, that the Beatles were "more popular than Jesus."[12] Other trends and bigger bands eclipsed the Beatles in less than a generation. John Lennon himself took a stab at being a visionary, a prophet, who appeared naked daily before Yoko Ono and friends in order to prophesy. His prophecies were incoherent and certainly never came to pass. Yoko, a member of the Beatles' close circle, later made a film, which symbolically said everything. The purpose of the film was to display naked rear ends, for world peace. Lucifer's kingdom, mentioned by Saul Alinsky at the outset of this book, which seemed so promising in both the Garden of Eden, and at the outset and development of modernity, could adopt this as its final disjointed statement. John and Yoko were not violent, but inane and pointless violence is another of the typical places where Lucifer's rebellion ends. It is an anodyne to the boredom of empty peace that is filled with nothing. A kingdom of boredom, savagery, and imbecility are poor payoffs. Can my grandfather and Saul Alinsky do no better?

---

11. Reagan's own advisers kept taking the phrase out of Reagan's speech (which he delivered in Berlin), and he kept putting it back in. He spoke this way against even what his people thought was "politic." The ensuing firestorm was most instructive. Not since Winston Churchill's "Iron Curtain" speech has a political speech aroused so much opposition. Commentators were horrified, and said, in way after way, that one cannot introduce this sort of moral language into "real politic." It is dangerous and foolish. Reagan's remark, and, indeed, the whole rest of that speech, amounted to a world political leader giving imprimatur to everything Solzhenitsyn had said. It contributed greatly to the tumbling down of the Soviets. They lost moral authority, even in their own eyes.

12. The full text of what John Lennon said was: "Christianity will go. It will vanish and shrink. I needn't argue about that. I'm right and I'll be proved right. We're more popular than Jesus now. I don't know which will go first, rock 'n' roll or Christianity. Jesus was all right but his disciples were thick and ordinary. It's them twisting it that ruins it for me."

"Who do people say the Son of Man is?" asked Jesus of the disciples one day. They gave all of the popular answers. "But what about you?" he asked. "Who do you say that I am?" (Matt 16:13b, 15). It is not sufficient to be done with Jesus by recounting what any crowd, ancient or modern say he is. He presses you; he presses my grandfather; he presses Saul Alinsky. An answer must be given. Blessed is the man who can say with Peter, "You are the Christ, the Son of the living of God." In another place in the Gospel of John, after Jesus has offended many in the crowds around him, and they have left, Jesus turns to his disciples and asks, "You do not want to leave too, do you?" (John 6:66–69). Again, Peter speaks for them all and declares that there is no one else to go to, there is nowhere else to go. Indeed, after one has met him, all other places become nothing. Come in. He bids you to come in. He welcomes you home.

12

Afterword

I AM NOT A professional philosopher. The truly technical side, especially of modern philosophy, is largely beyond me. When people start speaking in algebraic equations, my eyes begin to cross, and I am immediately lost. There may be a great deal that I have missed. Hopefully, though, I have some knack for seeing and intuiting larger philosophical issues, and I hope I have had a few things to say that may be helpful especially to "seekers," those looking for faith.

Anyone who knows about these things will quickly see that this little volume is a species of what has come to be termed "presuppositionalism." This, in and of itself, is no longer very interesting or controversial. It is now very broadly—indeed, almost universally—conceded in the world of the learned that everyone begins with some stance, some prejudice, some deep pre-theoretical commitment that shapes every word and thought. One no longer needs to fight very hard to convince people of this. Now that someone can say something illuminating along these lines is another matter. How successful I have been will be for other people to judge.

Behind almost everything I have said, there stands the thinking and work of Dr. Cornelius Van Til. I mentioned him only occasionally in the text. A certain inner ring mentality in my circles believe that merely saying his name, and repeating his rote formulas is a badge of "theological correctness." I wanted very much to avoid that feeling and that kind of name-dropping. I think it will take another generation before Van Til can be mentioned without hearing that echo, and before he can be interacted with more dispassionately, like one might now say, "as Pascal says," or "as Augustine reminds us." However, I have personally found this sort of easy familiarity is almost impossible with Van Til's name. There are too many passionate friends and enemies for it not to sound like a dogfight, or like choosing up sides, when his name is brought up. I do not think, in attempting to write a short book like this one, that it is helpful to come across sounding like a fellow traveler, or a propagandist for a circle of people. In my own experimentation in writing, that is always how it seemed to sound when I had written his name or quoted him. For this reason, I have largely left his name out of things. Let me record here my own personal debt to Van Til, lest I be justly accused of ingratitude. It is always difficult to evaluate a thinker too near his own lifetime, but I think that Van Til's real importance as a thinker is still largely unrecognized, and I think it is very great indeed. He did not have the gift of clarity, although he could use homespun illustrations of his thinking to great effect. He did, however, have a kind of metaphysical genius that was able to penetrate to first principles in a breathtaking way. I had the feeling after studying Van Til that he had ruined philosophy for me. He saw so clearly the overarching structure of human thought in its largest strokes, that I felt for some time that he had taken all the fun out of being able to learn anything genuinely new again. He revealed to me the underlying similarity of structure that is to be found almost everywhere in even the most diverse of thinkers.

I also owe a great debt of gratitude to Dr. John Frame who was one of Dr. Van Til's own students, and who was my professor while I studied theology at Westminster Theological Seminary a number of years ago. Van Til had personally passed off the scene by the time I showed up at Westminster. I had met him, and he was still alive, but he was a very old man by then and no longer an active teacher. I remember having the feeling that even if the opportunity had been given me, I would not have wanted to study directly under Van Til anyway. By the time I went to seminary, I had read most of Van Til's works, and I had worked very hard at understanding them. I knew, even apart from meeting him, that he did not exactly have the knack of making things clear or of cleaning up all the loose ends. John Frame distinctly did, however, and he had thought through most of the things that left me constantly baffled and scratching my head when I read Van Til. I'm not sure that Frame is Van Til's successor in a singular way, but he is a successor and perhaps the most significant one, and his gifts are a great compliment to Van Til's. Apart from a successor like Frame, a thinker like Van Til is either too easily overlooked, or too easily venerated. Frame has complained of the lack of a company of thinkers who will appreciatively but not uncritically interact with Van Til's contribution. He has left me with this ideal, and with whatever small gifts I have, I hope I can offer some positive interaction, application, and use of Van Til's thought along with Frame himself. I would never have written this little volume had it not been at Professor Frame's suggestion in the first place. I would never have persevered if not for his long, gentle encouragement to me along the way.

Bibliography

Adams, D. L. "Saul Alinsky and the Rise of Amorality in American Politics." *The New English Review,* January 2010. www.newenglishreview.org/DL_Adams/Saul_Alinsky_ and_the_Rise_of_Amorality_in_American_Politics/.

Alinsky, Saul David. *Rules for Radicals.* New York: Vintage, 1989.

Augustine. *Confessions.* Translated by Henry Chadwick. Oxford: Oxford University Press, 1992.

———. "On the Holy Trinity." *Christian Classics Ethereal Library.* Edited by Paul Schaff. http://www.ccel.org/ccel/schaff/npnf103.

B., Dick. *The Good Book and Big Book: A.A.s Roots in the Bible.* E-book. Sarasota, FL: First Edition Design, 2011.

———. *The Oxford Group and Alcoholics Anonymous.* E-book. Sarasota, FL: First Edition Design, 2011.

Barfield, Owen. *Saving the Appearances: A Study in Idolatry.* Middletown, CT: Wesleyan University Press, 1965.

Barth, Markus. *Justification: Pauline Texts Interpreted in the Light of the Old and New Testaments.* Grand Rapids: Eerdmans, 1971.

Berkhof, Hendrikus. *Christ and the Powers.* Translated by John H. Yoder. Scottdale, PA: Herald, 1962.

Berkeley, Jon. "Towards the End of Poverty." *The Economist,* June 1, 2013. http://www.economist.com/news/leaders/21578665-nearly-1-billion-people-have-been-taken-out-extreme-poverty-20-years-world-should-aim.

Bethell, Tom. *Eric Hoffer: The Longshoreman Philosopher.* Stanford, CA: Hoover Institution Press, Stanford University, 2012.

Bledsoe, Richard. "A Visit to Orthodoxy." *Revbledsoe's Weblog,* September 28, 2005. http://revbledsoe.wordpress.com/2009/02/21/entry-for-september-28-2005-a-visit-to-orthodoxy/.

Bloom, Allan. *Closing of the American Mind.* New York: Simon & Schuster, 1987.

Bonhoeffer, Dietrich. *Ethics.* Edited by Eberhard Bethge. Translated by Neville Horton Smith. New York: Macmillan, 1978.

Buckley, Michael. *The Origins of Modern Atheism.* New Haven: Yale University Press, 1987.

Calvin, John. *Institutes of the Christian Religion. Christian Classics Ethereal Library.* http://www.ccel.org/ccel/calvin/institutes.iii.ii.html.

Campbell, Keith, and Jean M. Twenge. *The Narcissism Epidemic: Living in the Age of Entitlement.* 1st ed. New York: Free Press, 2009.

Capon, Robert Farrar. *Bed and Board: Plain Talk About Marriage.* New York: Simon & Schuster, 1965.

BIBLIOGRAPHY

Carson, D. A. *The Gagging of God: Christianity Confronts Pluralism*. Grand Rapids: Zondervan, 1996.

Chambers, Whittaker. *Witness*. Chicago: Regnery Gateway, 1952.

Chesterton, G. K. *Orthodoxy*. Reprint. San Francisco: Ignatius, 1995.

———. *Saint Thomas Aquinas: "The Dumb Ox."* Garden City, NY: Doubleday Image, 1956.

Clifford, William K. "The Ethics of Belief." http://myweb.lmu.edu/tshanahan/Clifford-Ethics_of_Belief.html.

Cochrane, Charles Norris. *Christianity and Classical Culture: A Study of Thought and Action from Augustus to Augustine*. London: Oxford University Press, 1957.

Daniel, Prayson. "Anselm's Ontological Argument." Blog. *With All I Am: Think, Reason, Follow*. http://withalliamgod.wordpress.com/2013/04/25/anselms-ontological-argument/.

Ferguson, Kitty. *The Fire in the Equations: Science, Religion, and the Search for God*. Grand Rapids: Eerdmans, 1994.

Flew, Antony, and Roy Abraham Varghese. *There Is a God*. E-book. New York: HarperCollins, 2009.

Fukuyama, Francis. *The End of History and the Last Man*. New York: Free Press, 1992.

Gilder, George F. *Wealth and Poverty*. New York: Basic Books, 1981.

Glasser, William. *Reality Therapy: A New Approach to Psychiatry*. New York: Harper & Row, 1975.

Golding, William. *The Lord of the Flies*. New York: Coward-McCann, 1962.

Goldman, David P. *It's Not the End of the World, It's Just the End of You and Me: The Great Extinction of the Nations*. New York: RVP, 2011.

Goodman, Alana. "The Hillary Letters." *The Washington Free Beacon*, September 24, 2014. http://freebeacon.com/politics/the-hillary-letters/.

Grimsley, Ronald. "Rousseau, Jean-Jacques." *The Encyclopedia of Philosophy*. 1967. Reprint, New York: Macmillan, 1972.

Harmon, Katherine. "How Important is Physical Contact with Your Infant?" *Scientific American*, May 6, 2010. http://www.scientificamerican.com/article/infant-touch/.

Heidegger, Martin. *What Is This Called Thinking?* 1st ed. New York: Harper & Row, 1968.

Hoeksema, Herman. *Reformed Dogmatics*. Grand Rapids: Reformed Free, 1966.

Hooper, Walter. "Truth about Anscombe v. C. S. Lewis." *The Telegraph*, January 11, 2001. http://www.telegraph.co.uk/comment/letters/4258502/Truth-about-Anscombe-v-C-S-Lewis.html.

Howard, Peter. *Frank Buchman's Secret*. London: Heinemann, 1961.

Hume, David. *A Treatise of Human Nature*. Edited by L. A. Selby-Bigge and P. H. Nidditch. Oxford: Clarendon, 1978.

Jaki, Stanley. *Science and Creation: From Eternal Cycles to an Oscillating Universe*. New York: Science History Publications, 1974.

Jones, E. Stanley. *Along the Indian Road*. London: Hodder & Stoughton, 1939.

———. *Mahatma Gandhi: An Interpretation*. London: Hodder & Stoughton, 1948.

Jordan, James. "Biblical Horizons Newsletter No. 15: The Dominion Trap." *Biblical Horizons*, July 1990. http://www.biblicalhorizons.com/biblical-horizons/no-15-the-dominion-trap/.

———. "Rebellion, Tyranny, and Dominion in the Book of Genesis." In *Tactics of Christian Resistance. Christianity & Civilization*, edited by Gary North, 3:38–80. Tyler, TX: Geneva Divinity School Press, 1983.

BIBLIOGRAPHY

Keil, C. F., and F. Delitzsch. *The Pentateuch*. Translated by James Martin. Vol. 1. Grand Rapids: Eerdmans, 1973.

Kilpatrick, William. *Why Johnny Can't Tell Right from Wrong*. New York: Simon & Schuster, 1992.

Leithart, Peter. *Deep Comedy*. Moscow, ID: Canon, 2006.

Lewis, C. S. *The Abolition of Man*. New York: MacMillan, 1947.

———. *Mere Christianity*. New York: Macmillan, 1960.

———. *Miracles: A Preliminary Study*. 18th ed. New York: Macmillan, 1977.

———. "Modern Theology and Biblical Criticism." In *The Essential C. S. Lewis*, edited by Lyle Dorsett, 349–60. New York: Touchstone, 1996.

———. *A Preface to Paradise Lost*. New York: Oxford University Press, 1979.

Maritain, Jacques. *Distinguish to Unite or Degrees of Knowledge*. New York: Scribners, 1959.

Maritain, Raissa. *We Have Been Friends Together: Memoirs*. New York: Longmans, Green, 1942.

Marx, Karl. *Capital: A Critique of Political Economy*. New York: Modern Library, 1906.

Marx, Karl, and Friedrich Engels. *The Communist Manifesto*. New York: International Publishers, 1848.

Muggeridge, Malcolm. "Does England Really Need a Queen?" *The Gargoyle: Journal of the Malcolm Muggeridge Society* 16 (2007) 3–11.

Nault, Jean Charles. "Acedia: Enemy of Spiritual Joy." *Communio: International Catholic Review* 31 (2004) 236–58.

Newbigin, Lesslie. *Truth and Authority in Modernity*. Valley Forge, PA: Trinity Press International, 1996.

Nietszche, Friedrich. *On the Genealogy of Morals*. Translated by Walter Kaufmann and R. J. Hollingdale. New York: Random House, 1969.

Osborn, E. F. "Aristotle." In *The Encyclopedia of Philosophy*, edited by Paul Edwards, 151–64. New York: Macmillan, 1967.

Parker, William R. and Elaine St. Johns Dare. *Prayer Can Change Your Life: Experiments and Techniques in Prayer Therapy*. Englewood Cliffs, NJ: Prentice Hall, 1957.

Pascal, Blaise. *Pensees*. Translated by Roger Ariew. Indianapolis: Hackett, 2005.

Picard, Max. *Flight from God*. Translated by Marrianne Kuschnizky and J. M. Cameron. Chicago: Regnery, 1951.

Plantinga, Alvin. *God and Other Minds: A Study of the Rational Justification of Belief in God*. Ithaca, NY: Cornell University Press, 1967.

———. *Warranted Christian Belief*. E-book. Oxford: Oxford University Press, 2000.

———. *Where the Conflict Really Lies: Science, Religion, and Naturalism*. Oxford: Oxford University Press, 2011.

"Pleasantville (film)." *Wikipedia*. http://en.wikipedia.org/wiki/Pleasantville_(film).

Polanyi, Michael. *Personal Knowledge: Towards a Post-Critical Philosophy*. 16th ed. Chicago: University of Chicago Press, 2004.

———. *Science, Faith, and Society*. University of Durham Riddell Memorial Lectures, 18. London: Oxford University Press, 1946.

Poythress, Vern S. *Redeeming Science: A God-Centered Approach*. Wheaton, IL: Crossway, 2006.

Rosenstock-Huessy, Eugen. *The Christian Future: Or The Modern Mind Outrun*. New York: Harper, 1966.

Rousseau, Jean-Jacques. *Confessions*. Translated by S. W. Orson. Project Gutenburg, 1896. www.gutenburg.org/ebooks/3913.

Rushdoony, R. J. *The One and the Many*. Fairfax, VA: Thoburn, 1978.

Sartre, Jean-Paul. *Nausea*. Translated by Lloyd Alexander. New York: New Directions, 1964.

Schaff, Philip. *The Creeds of Christendom*. Vol. 3. Grand Rapids: Baker, 1998.

Scheler, Max. *Ressentiment*. Translated by Manfred S. Frings. Marquette Studies in Philosophy, 7. Milwaukee, WI: Marquette University Press, 1998.

Seuss, Dr. *The Cat in The Hat*. New York: Random House, 1957.

Sproul, R. C. *If There Is a God, Why Are There Atheists?* Wheaton, IL: Tyndale, 1989.

Steer, Roger. *Delighted in God*. Wheaton, IL: Harold Shaw, 1981.

Szasz, Thomas. *The Myth of Mental Illness*. New York: Harper & Row, 1974.

Tournier, Paul. *A Place For You*. New York: Harper & Row, 1968.

TWC. "Is Naturalism Self-Defeating?" *Naturalism.Org*, March 2007. http://naturalism.org/plantinga.htm.

Twenge, Jean M. *Generation Me: Why Today's Young Americans are More Confident, Assertive, Entitled—and More Miserable Than Ever Before*. New York: Free Press, 2006.

Van Heijenoort, J. "Godel's Theorem." In *Encyclopedia of Philosophy*, vol. 3. New York: Macmillan, 1967.

Van Til, Cornelius. *A Christian Theory of Knowledge*. Philadelphia: Presbyterian & Reformed, 1969.

———. *The Defense of the Faith*. 3rd ed. Philadelphia: Presbyterian & Reformed, 1967.

———. *Psychology of Religion*. Philadelphia: Westminster Theological Seminary, 1960.

Warfield, B. B. *The Inspiration and Authority of the Bible*. Philadelphia: Presbyterian & Reformed, 1948.

———. "Misconception of Jesus, and Blasphemy of the Son of Man." In *Biblical and Theological Studies*, 196–237. Philadelphia: Presbyterian & Reformed, 1968.

Wolfe, Tom. "Radical Chic: That Party at Lenny's." *New York Magazine*, June 1970. http://nymag.com/news/features/46170/.

Zahavi, Dan. "Schizophrenia and Self-Awareness." *Philosophy, Psychiatry, & Psychology* 8.4 (2001) 339–41.